Over thirty years as a pastor, I've found that bitterness toward God is *often the primary barrier* to accepting His salvation and trusting His guidance on a daily basis. I know of no one better suited than R. T. Kendall to address this deep hurt in so many lives. I'm so grateful for this book.

—RICK WARREN
PASTOR, SADDLEBACK CHURCH
AUTHOR, *THE PURPOSE–DRIVEN LIFE*

R. T. Kendall is a Christian leader for whom I have the greatest respect. A best-selling author, preacher, and theologian, he is never afraid to tackle the big issues, such as the reality of suffering and the struggles of life. I commend this book to you.

—NICKY GUMBEL
VICAR, HOLY TRINITY BROMPTON
LONDON, ENGLAND

Forgiving God for not intervening in times of suffering and trouble is taboo for many writers, but not for R. T. Kendall. What he writes so brilliantly not only helps us spiritually, but it also helps us psychologically.

—TONY CAMPOLO, PhD
PROFESSOR EMERITUS OF SOCIOLOGY
EASTERN UNIVERSITY

R. T. Kendall writes as he speaks—with depth, conviction, and the ability to surprise the reader/listener into a reevaluation of attitude, conviction, and lifestyle. If you value a comfortable, private, and convenient life, then this book is not for you. If you hunger for more of God, long to go on with Him, and seek that life ahead might be lived in the closest and most intimate fellowship with Jesus, then this is a book you must read. I cannot offer more than deep gratitude to R. T. Kendall for rocking the boat and disturbing my life—yet again!

—Rev. Dr. Clive Calver
Senior Pastor, Walnut Hill
Community Church
Former President, World Relief

The greatest puzzle in the universe is the way God seems to betray us. No one can explain it just yet, but RT shows us how to cope. Highly recommended.

—Dr. Michael Eaton
Nairobi, Kenya

If you feel let down or disappointed with God, this book is a "must read" for you. Once again RT has dealt with a tough subject magnificently!

—Lyndon Bowring
Executive Chairman, CARE

This is quite simply the most important book RT has ever written. I have enjoyed his writing in the past and often found it challenging and sometimes disagreed with it, but I never failed to be stimulated by what he produces. This, however, is on a different level. RT is dealing with one of the most pernicious and subtle sins of the Christian life—resentment and unforgiveness directed against God, sometimes conscious, sometimes unconscious. This book is wise, penetrating, asking questions that dig deep into us on a personal level. It is, in fact, personal as well from his understanding. He confesses he knows about this issue inside. It is powerful because it doesn't pull any punches. He analyses all the areas of resentment and reasons for unforgiveness.

Finally, it is intensely practical in that it gives us ways to deal with the issue in our own lives and shows us how to move forward. This book could change your life, liberating you to become the person God has always dreamed of you being, free at last from the chains of unforgiveness toward God. A magnificent work of spiritual diagnosis and a powerful prescription for health.

—Eric Delve
Vicar, St. Luke's Church
Maidstone, Kent, England

Dr. R. T. Kendall's trilogy on forgiveness has reached its apex with this volume on forgiving God. He builds from the solid foundation of God's faithfulness, purity, and perfection, and the eternal truth that God cannot and has not done wrong at any time. This book will set you free, and you will never "blame God" again for circumstances and situations that come your way. This volume is destined to take its place among the Christian classics. "Free at last" will be the enduring cry of those who read and reap the truth of this book.

—O. S. Hawkins
President/CEO
GuideStone Financial Resources

I had read only a few lines into the manuscript of this book when I thought of a dear Christian couple who lost their two-year-old daughter to cancer. When the light went out of that tiny body they walked away from God. The message in this book will help bring them—and many others like them—back to life and love again.

—CHARLES CARRIN
CHARLES CARRIN MINISTRIES

R. T. Kendall is one of the most remarkable men I have ever known. When I introduce him at our conferences, I observe, "RT goes to England every two weeks and writes a book every Thursday!" Well, perhaps not that remarkable, but I think I have read everything he has written and up comes another. I cannot keep myself from reading his latest because I feel that the latest is probably his best. It may be true of this one as I have never been disappointed in one yet. RT seems to have the knack of taking a difficult or obscure subject and mining the riches few suspicioned were there. Good work, RT!

—JACK TAYLOR
DIMENSIONS MINISTRIES
MELBOURNE, FLORIDA

TOTALLY
FOR GIVING
GOD

TOTALLY FOR GIVING GOD

R. T. KENDALL

CHARISMA
HOUSE

Most CHARISMA HOUSE BOOK GROUP products are available at special quantity discounts for bulk purchase for sales promotions, premiums, fund-raising, and educational needs. For details, write Charisma House Book Group, 600 Rinehart Road, Lake Mary, Florida 32746, or telephone (407) 333-0600.

TOTALLY FORGIVING GOD by R. T. Kendall
Published by Charisma House
Charisma Media/Charisma House Book Group
600 Rinehart Road
Lake Mary, Florida 32746
www.charismahouse.com

Unless otherwise noted, all Scripture quotations are from the Holy Bible, New International Version. Copyright ©1973, 1978, 1984, International Bible Society. Used by permission.

Scripture quotations marked ESV are from the Holy Bible, English Standard Version. Copyright © 2001 by Crossway Bibles, a division of Good News Publishers. Used by permission.

Scripture quotations marked HCSB are from the Holman Christian Standard Bible. Copyright © 1999, 2000, 2002, 2003 by Holman Bible Publishers, Nashville Tennessee. All rights reserved.

Scripture quotations marked JB are from The Jerusalem Bible, copyright © 1966, 1967, 1968 by Darton, Longman and Todd Ltd and Doubleday, a division of Random House, Inc.

Scripture quotations marked KJV are from the King James Version of the Bible.

Scripture quotations marked NKJV are from the New King James Version of the Bible. Copyright © 1979, 1980, 1982 by Thomas Nelson, Inc., publishers. Used by permission.

Scripture quotations marked RSV are from the Revised Standard Version of the Bible. Copyright © 1946, 1952, 1971 by the Division of Christian Education of the National Council of the Churches of Christ in the USA. Used by permission.

Scripture quotations marked TLB are from The Living Bible. Copyright © 1971. Used by permission of Tyndale House Publishers, Inc., Wheaton, IL 60189. All rights reserved.

Cover design by Justin Evans
Design Director: Bill Johnson

Visit the author's website at www.rtkendallministries.com.

Library of Congress Cataloging-in-Publication Data:
Kendall, R. T.
Totally forgiving God / R.T. Kendall. -- 1st ed.
p. cm.
ISBN 978-1-61638-854-6 (trade paper) -- ISBN 978-1-61638-858-4 (e-book)
1. Suffering--Religious aspects--Christianity. 2. Trust in God. 3. Spirituality. 4. Forgiveness--Religious aspects--Christianity. 5. Forgiveness of sin. I. Title.

BV4909.K44 2012
248.8'6--dc23

2012011704

While the author has made every effort to provide accurate telephone numbers and Internet addresses at the time of publication, neither the publisher nor the author assumes any responsibility for errors or for changes that occur after publication.

First edition

12 13 14 15 16—9 8 7 6 5 4 3 2 1
Printed in the United States of America

To Marilyn

CONTENTS

FOREWORD

I JUST CAN'T SEEM to forgive God" is a common phrase I've heard in ministry over the years. Whether experiencing personal grief or physical suffering, we all have a propensity to blame God for circumstances beyond our control—and as such find it hard to "forgive" Him. I've experienced it in my own life.

I will always remember the way my sister died. She was barely a young adult when she was diagnosed with cancer for the second time. We, as a family, travailed the challenge of watching her as a twelve-year-old suffer from a rare form of skin cancer. The chemotherapy, the disfiguring surgery, and all the accompanying challenges were realities in our everyday lives. As a relatively new believer, my mother deeply struggled with how God could allow such a thing. As a new believer myself, I prayed—believing the Scriptures—for God to heal my sister Betty. She got better—for nine years.

Yet, ultimately, God, in His infinite wisdom, chose not to heal Betty.

I remember the day, June of 1986, when we stood by her bedside as she closed her eyes for the last time and died. My mother dropped out of church and the faith that day for seven years. I struggled, never finding a satisfying answer to the question "Why?", but I trusted that God had a divine purpose. Both Mom and I had to confront the issue we *perceived* as God's unfairness.

My mother avoided confrontation with God for seven years. Mom stayed away from church and away from Christians. She could not understand (and still does not understand) why God would allow such a thing to happen. But through the love of a particular family and various friends, Mom eventually came to the conclusion that she must let go of her anger toward God. In a sense, she had to forgive God.

My own grief required less time but was equally tormenting. I remember, after Betty died, driving to the shore of a nearby beach and yelling at God. Honestly I used words that one should not use when addressing a holy God. I demanded answers.

The answers my soul craved never came. God rejected my wisdom in favor of His own. He did not give me the answers I wanted, but He gave me something better. He gave me Himself instead.

I remember that night—among many others—quoting Proverbs 3:5–6, which says "Trust in the LORD with all your heart, and do not rely on your own understanding; think about Him in all your ways, and He will guide you on the right paths" (HCSB).

Since this is an issue so close to my heart, I am encouraged to see my friend R. T. Kendall tackle this issue head-on. Of course the idea of "forgiving God" will certainly ruffle some feathers, but the point here is so clear: God is perfect, and just yet our hearts often hold bitterness toward Him—and we need to let that bitterness go and trust God.

RT understands that God does not need to be forgiven. He is, as RT explains, perfectly holy, just, righteous, and wise in all of His dealings with us. God only desires and provides the best for His people, though we may not realize it at the time.

Also, RT knows that God has done nothing wrong and is not in need of our pardon or recompense. RT holds to a high view of God, and nothing could be further from the truth. Yet because we live in a fallen and broken world, because we agonize over suffering, and because of our limited knowledge, we become angry with God. RT exhorts readers to repent from sinful anger toward God and break free from its bondage.

Yes, on that day many years ago, I had to let go of my bitterness—and my guess is that many of you may have picked up this book precisely because you feel you need to forgive God.

With pastoral insight and keen theological observations, RT helps us to see not that God needs to be forgiven, but that we need be repentant. Glory be to God for a friend like R. T. Kendall who desires to see sinners like you and me be reconciled to an omnipotent, omniscient, sovereign God.

—ED STETZER
PRESIDENT, LIFEWAY RESEARCH

SPECIAL RECOMMENDATION
FROM THE
UNITED KINGDOM

IN A HUNDRED years' time when people look back on the literature that molded the Christian generation of today, I have no doubt that a book written by R. T. Kendall almost twenty years ago will be on the list. It is called *Total Forgiveness*. It was an uncomfortable book—a book that called us to do the unthinkable: to actually forgive those who had hurt us deeply, irrespective of their repentance toward us. But as if that were not enough, it urged us to pray that those we forgave may never know how much we had suffered at their hands. And it asked us to play our part in making sure that no one ever heard of how they had wronged us.

For those of us who wanted our enemies to wake up one day in a bath of sweat caused by the guilt of the crimes they had committed against us, this book was not good news. And yet as we read it and its truth seeped into our souls, we began to believe that, in fact, the only way to freedom was for us to learn to forgive as R. T. Kendall urged.

That book touched the lives of so many people. It brought hope to men and women in prison cells. It urged squabbling churches to think again—to look beyond the petty hurts that were clutched to chests so dearly. It allowed married couples to turn away from yesterdays filled with a thousand hurts and to look ahead to a new tomorrow.

And then came the book *How to Forgive Ourselves—Totally*, and suddenly we all realized what we had always suspected: that although forgiving others is hard, there is another who needs the touch of grace—someone on whom we are often much harder.

Perhaps R. T. Kendall should have stopped there. He'd given birth to two great books that blessed thousands across the world; books that, although difficult, were hardly controversial. But he didn't. And the book you now hold in your hands has a title that will, at first, shock its readers more than it blesses them. "How on earth," they will say, "can God— the Holy One—possibly need *our* forgiveness?" Perhaps they are right. Perhaps, with this latest book, R. T. Kendall has jumped off the cliff that lies at the edge of reason and fallen into the void of foolishness.

But will everyone think this? The mother who believed her son was healed of cancer thanked God for the miracle, and a year later wept at his graveside? The man who has just had the letter that tells him he won't have a job next Monday? The woman who has trusted all her life that one day God would grant her a husband and now, as later life dawns, fears her dream will never be fulfilled? Will they say that R. T. Kendall has lost his mind?

No. Millions of the broken and the disappointed, the letdown and the disillusioned, will agree that sometimes, at least, it *feels as though God needs to be forgiven.*

But this book is important not just for them. The truth is that none of us can make it to the end of our Christian lives—can run the course, fight the fight, grasp the prize—unless we are willing to live with and perhaps even embrace what R. T. Kendall calls "the betrayal barrier."

Into a world that bombards us with the message that following Christ will make us rich, healthy, or just about anything else we dream of being, comes a book that takes us into the life of Habakkuk, the Old Testament prophet who struggled with the dilemma that faces each of us today: How do we go on believing when "the fig tree does not bud and there are no grapes on the vines"? How do we hold on to faith when "the olive crop fails and the fields produce no food"? In short, how do we love God when life screams at us that He is either impotent to act or uncaring of our pain? If you want an easy answer, stop reading now—put the book down. The world's libraries are filled with far easier books than this. But if you are ready to at least begin to grapple with the greatest problem that men and women face in loving God, then begin the journey.

Begin the journey that may end with you leaning on the fences of empty sheep pens, weeping at vines bereft of fruit, and gazing at fields that show no hint of the promised harvest. Begin the journey that may end with you saying along with Habakkuk: "Still will I rejoice in God." And if you reach that place, R. T. Kendall says you will know two things for sure: first, that you truly love God, and second, that you are greatly loved *by Him.* In fact, the whole book might be summed up in two lines, which come toward the end:

> Whatever has happened to you was not when He had
> His head turned. He was looking straight at you.

Can *you* totally forgive God?

Begin the journey...

—Rob Parsons
Chairman and Founder, Care for the Family
United Kingdom

PREFACE

W HEN MY BOOK *How to Forgive Ourselves—Totally* was published a few years ago, a very dear friend of mine said, "RT, I know what should be the title of your next book." "What is that?" I asked. "*Totally Forgiving God*," he replied. "Oh, dear," I swallowed. My immediate thought, I am ashamed to admit, was about what the critics will say when they see the title but won't read the book. But in a day or two after that I knew in my heart he was right and that I should pursue this idea and write the book.

But it hasn't been easy. I have possibly given more thought and prayer to this than any book I have written. I try always to be careful, but with this grave subject I needed to be doubly sure that I knew what I was talking about. People ask, "How long does it take to write a book?" The answer is, "It all depends." Some books take weeks; some take months. This book has taken five years to write. I have sought the counsel of close friends with whom I have shared the manuscript. Somerset Maugham said that when people ask for criticism, they really want praise! True. But I needed a lot more than praise when it came to this book; I needed all the criticism and help I could get. Several friends have read this manuscript, but I am deeply indebted particularly to Ed Stetzer, for writing the foreword, Lyndon Bowring, Dr. Michael Eaton, and, most of all, to Rob Parsons, who has done us a singular favor by writing the special recommendation to this book. Thank you, Rob. Your help with this book and many others I have written over the years has been incalculable.

When I wrote *Total Forgiveness*, I had no idea that there would be a need for *How to Forgive Ourselves—Totally*. But there was. This will (as far as I know) be the last in this mini series of titles.

This book is dedicated to my baby sister, Marilyn, who has undergone far more hurt and suffering than I have known. I pray it will encourage you, Marilyn.

It is my fervent, earnest prayer that every reader will be warmly blessed as they read what follows. God bless you all.

—R. T. Kendall

www.rtkendallministries.com

INTRODUCTION

I have seen something else under the sun: The race is not to the swift or the battle to the strong, nor does food come to the wise or wealth to the brilliant or favor to the learned; but time and chance happen to them all. Moreover, no man knows when his hour will come: As fish are caught in a cruel net, or birds are taken in a snare, so men are trapped by evil times that fall unexpectedly upon them.

—ECCLESIASTES 9:11–12

Life's not fair.

—JOHN FITZGERALD KENNEDY (1917–1963)

IN FEBRUARY 1953, when I was seventeen, the class I was attending at the Ashland, Kentucky, senior high school was suddenly interrupted. The teacher called me out and said I had a phone call waiting for me in the principal's office. It was my from my uncle, who said, "RT, your mother has had a stroke and has been taken to the hospital. Your dad is on the way to take you there, so go outside and wait for him." I replied, "Is she going to be OK?" "I think your mother is very sick," he said. Moments later I got into the car with my dad as our Nazarene pastor drove us hurriedly to the hospital, where I saw my mother paralyzed on one side of her body.

For the next eight weeks we waited day and night for her to improve. All our friends and loved ones were praying for her. At least five people—known for their faithfulness—anointed her with oil to be healed. Some of them said they prayed through, meaning that God witnessed that my mother would be healed. My dad, the most godly man I ever knew, woke me up one morning with joy in his heart; God had just shown him that my mother would be healed. He based this on his reading from Psalm 6:8–9: "The LORD hath heard the voice of my weeping. The LORD hath heard my supplication; the LORD will receive my prayer" (KJV). I myself received also what I believed to be a word from the Lord that she would be healed, "Wait on the LORD: be of good courage, and he shall strengthen thine heart: wait, I say, on the LORD" (Ps. 27:14, KJV).

There was no doubt in my mind that God revealed to me and others that my mother would be healed and would not die.

Eight weeks later the members of my high school band (I played the oboe) had journeyed by train to Washington DC where we had been invited to play at the annual Cherry Blossom Festival. My mother insisted that I go. On the morning we arrived, April 8, 1953, I telephoned my aunt (who lived in Washington) merely to say I was in town. She said, "Where are you?" I explained I was in a restaurant having breakfast with other band students. She said, "Don't leave." I asked, "Why?" At first she would not tell me, but then she said, "Your mother passed away this morning."

I remember it as if it were yesterday. Later that same day I had my first plane ride—Aunt Freda went with me on a plane journey back to Ashland. When I entered our house, several members of our church were present. My dad fell on my shoulders, sobbing. The funeral was two days later. It was an event from which I have never fully recovered. Apart from his personal sorrow and the care of my little sister, Marilyn—born two years previously—my dad's chief concern was my own faith. He feared I would lose my faith in all this. I didn't. But the death of my mother had an impact on me that shaped my emotions, my thinking, and my expectancy from that day to this.

My dad would say in those days, "God is too wise to err and too kind to be unmerciful." I believed that then, and I believe it today.

The experience of losing my mother when I was a teenager does not qualify me to write this book. What I went through was a drop in the bucket compared to suffering and hurts and injustices others—and perhaps you—have experienced. I write out of a background of fifty-seven years of ministry, during which time I have been the pastor of five churches, my last being Westminster Chapel, where I was the minister for exactly twenty-five years. But that disappointment from thinking my mother would be healed owing to Psalm 27:14 was my first hint that God could allow me to think a certain way—and I be totally wrong. Psalm 27:14 says nothing, of course, about healing. But to me it did—at the time. It prepared me in some measure to be able to sympathize with people who have been hurt, sometimes disillusioned, by the God they so trusted in—only to feel utterly betrayed by Him.

About fifteen years ago the evangelical psychologist Dr. James Dobson called on me in my vestry at Westminster Chapel: "RT, I am writing a book on the subject when God doesn't make sense. Do you have any thoughts on this?"

The truth is, I did. Whereas most of Dr. Dobson's books are outside the realm of my expertise, his new title was right up my street. I began to share with him my embryonic thinking regarding the betrayal barrier that Christians sooner or later face. A few years after *When God Doesn't Make Sense* was first published, which Dr. Dobson had kindly dedicated to me, a new edition was planned. I was invited this time to write the foreword to it, and in it I unfolded a few more of my thoughts on the betrayal barrier and breaking the betrayal barrier that had become a part of Dr. Dobson's book. But I have felt for a long time that I would write a book of my own, enlarging on this idea. So when I conceived of writing the present book, *Totally Forgiving God,* I decided that this book would elaborate to some extent on the concept of God seemingly betraying us. My point is this. It was these insights, far more than the death of my mother, that has persuaded me that I should write the book you now hold in your hands.

The ability to forgive God comes down mainly to one thing: understanding the God of the Bible and His ways. The key to forgiving God is knowing His ways—and accepting them.

It is my sincere prayer that you will be encouraged as you read on and that you yourself will come to the place (if you have needed to do so)—sooner than later—that you *totally* forgive God for whatever it was that He allowed to happen in your life that led to your anger, hurt, frustration, or disillusionment. My aim in this book is to restore your faith in God's integrity and existence; that you will come to see for yourself that He exists and that He rewards those who seek Him (Heb. 11:6). He is worth seeking, and His reward is worth waiting for.

Totally Forgiving *God*?

The title of this book would suggest that God might be guilty of something—and that one should forgive Him. Is such a suggestion justified?

I must therefore explain why I have chosen to write this book. There is nobody on the planet who has not suffered to some degree in the world God created—into which sin entered—and the one He sustains. It is a wicked world, a world filled with suffering, injustice, and evil to overflowing. There is famine, war, earthquakes, tornadoes, hurricanes, tsunamis, wicked governments, corrupt financial institutions, poverty, racial prejudice, and disease. God could have prevented such from happening in the first place, and He could have intervened to stop any evil at any time.

In addition to situations in the world, we all have been hurt in varying degrees—whether being personally mistreated, taken advantage of, deceived, been in an accident, endured suffering through illness, losing a job, losing a loved one prematurely, losing a friend, or being falsely accused. This is to say nothing of those who have been raped, sexually abused, robbed, or given an unjust verdict by a corrupt judge.

God could have stopped any of these evils at any time in the entire world.

What is more, being a believer does not exempt one from suffering. Becoming a Christian does not remove one from pain. Bad things happen to Christians; good things happen to those who not only are unbelievers but who also do great evil in this world. President John F. Kennedy used to say, "Life's not fair."[1]

God allows this. He could stop it. After all, God by definition is unlimited in power and knowledge. He sees injustices and extreme suffering happening every day and apparently does nothing. According to James, whoever knows the right thing to do and fails to do it, for him it is sin (James 4:17). It seems to us that the right thing to do would be to stop evil! But God doesn't stop it. Why?

That is why I have written this book.

I will be as clear as I know how as I wind up this introduction so you will know exactly where I am coming from.

First, I honestly do not believe God is guilty of anything wrong. He has nothing to answer for. You will ask, "Then why do we need to forgive Him?" I will give three reasons that will be elaborated on in this book:

1. We must not be governed by our limited perception of Him—supposing that we are qualified to judge Him.

2. We forgive Him not because He is guilty, but because we choose to affirm Him as He is revealed in the Bible.

3. We must set Him free—letting Him totally off the hook—until the day arrives when every knee shall bow and every tongue confess that Jesus Christ is Lord to the glory of God the Father (Phil. 2:9–11).

By totally forgiving *God*, I mean the God of the Bible, the God who is revealed in the Old and New Testaments. There will be those who do not accept God as being unlimited in power and knowledge. Such people will not likely believe in the infallibility of Holy Scripture—which I do. They wish to maintain a belief in God, but it is not always the God of the Bible they want to believe in. A part of this book will focus on God and His *ways*.

A few years ago I wrote a book called *The Anointing: Yesterday, Today, Tomorrow*. I invited an old friend—a man highly esteemed in the theological world—to write a foreword to that book. He turned me down. I was quite devastated. I could think of nothing else for days. But he did no wrong at all by refusing to commend my book. He was being true to himself. I had to forgive him. It would be inappropriate for me to criticize him for his decision. He had his reasons. I was deeply hurt, yes. But he was not guilty of anything but being himself. This illustration of how I had to forgive my old friend does not begin to compare to the way

God remains true to Himself, but He must be forgiven when we are disappointed or feel betrayed.

I write this book to set you free. By your setting *God* free, you will be free. I guarantee it. Never have I written a book with such painful thought and care. I have been working on it for years. It is my conviction that this will lead you to not only a spiritual breakthrough in understanding God but also a breakthrough in your own mind and spirit. I pray as I write these lines that the Holy Spirit will enable you to perceive what is intended by what I have written; that you will not misinterpret, misapply, or misunderstand what follows but will have an emancipation from bewilderment or any bitterness; and that you will fall in love with the Bible and the God who gave it to us. He is worth seeking, and His reward is worth waiting for.

PART ONE

Our Perspective

O Lord... you have put me in the lowest pit, in the darkest depths... the darkness is my closest friend.
                                        —Psalm 88:1, 6, 18

All looks yellow to the jaundiced eye.
                                        —Alexander Pope (1688–1744)

CHAPTER ONE

The Dilemma

Judge nothing before the appointed time; wait till the Lord comes. He will bring to light what is hidden in darkness and will expose the motives of men's hearts. At that time each will receive his praise from God.

—1 CORINTHIANS 4:5

I do not know how the great loving Father will bring out light at last, but He knows, and He will do it.

—DAVID LIVINGSTONE (1813–1873)

AFTER FIFTY-SEVEN YEARS of Christian ministry, I have observed and experienced countless enigmas. I have more questions I want to see answered in heaven than you could imagine. For example, I will never forget preaching the funeral sermon of a gifted child who had such a brilliant future, and shortly after that watching old people who don't know their names live on and on. I have often prayed with the most beautiful and worthy people who remain unmarried (against their wish) and have seen countless others marry (and wish they hadn't). I have seen some of my warmest and most selfless supporters being taken home to heaven while some of those who were not very appreciative of my ministry thrive under God's apparent blessing. I have known people in the ministry who I felt should be under the just judgment of God but who flourished instead, and those who were faithful and godly who have never been very successful.

I can't explain it, but I have been continually surprised to see how many apparently dysfunctional parents have produced the most productive, amazing, and godly children. On the other hand I have watched those parents who seemed to me to be the nearest to perfection one can imagine, and how many, to their dismay, watched their children grow up to reject the faith, marry the most unsuitable mates, and end up tragically. I recall one godly layman who prayed daily for years and years that his two children would not fall in love with the wrong person. In one case his prayer was clearly answered; one child seemed to be so extremely blessed and enjoyed a long, fruitful marriage. But the other child went through two divorces and has known anything but marital bliss.

How could these things be? Why does God let people exist with Alzheimer's or dementia who cannot possibly live productive lives? Why does God appear to bless certain flamboyant ministries who uphold questionable teaching but not seemingly bless others who have sought to be sound, self-effacing, and honest? Why would God answer the prayers of a godly layman for one of his children and not the other? These are questions I expect to have answered in heaven.

Some of the words of Solomon seem so ironic if not cynical. But if one lives long enough, he or she too will have to agree with this observation: "Righteous men who get what the wicked deserve, and wicked men who get what the righteous deserve" (Eccles. 8:14). So after all is said and done, we must all do our best and then trust the mercy of God—and be thankful when that mercy is manifest in our lives and in our children. If any of us enjoy any accomplishments, they will have come by the sheer grace of God.

My Aim in Writing This Book

I write this book as a follower of Jesus Christ rather than as a theologian, pastor, or evangelist. My aim in writing this book is to uphold the God of the Bible as faithfully as I can while also sharing with you as honestly as I can some of the things I have learned and observed. I am sure you have found out that life is not all black or white. You may even have personal stories, which, if I knew them, would make better illustrations than I have in writing this book. Perhaps you too have lived through disappointment, disillusionment, rejection, and betrayal. I am not writing a book that gives you a rosy picture of the Christian life, of Christians, the church, or of high-profile leaders whom God has used. The best of men are men at best.

For some reason I have always had a tendency to be a hero worshiper. From the age of ten I began to admire Joe DiMaggio, the baseball player of the New York Yankees. I even combed my hair like he did and tried to smile like he did. I read the sports page every morning with anxiety to see if he hit a home run the day before. If his batting average was up, so was my spirit. He could do no wrong in my eyes. Twenty years later I had the chance to meet him. After I shook his hand, I was as excited as if I were a ten-year-old child. I still love reading anything I can about him.

Unfortunately I carried this tendency into my life in the church. Even those I learned to love and admire let me down. From an early age my dad introduced me to famous preachers, and I began to look up to them. I hero-worshiped many preachers. But little by little I began to get a different picture of some of them. I began to hear stories of inconsistent living, their upholding high standards for their followers but living hypocritically in secret. Some of these people became friends, some very close friends. I learned a long time ago—years before we went to England—every person I began to admire a little bit too much sooner or later disappointed me.

It is sad that some young people who are preparing for ministry in the church get completely disillusioned when they see older Christians who disappoint them, especially if their mentor was flawed. I know some of those who gave up the idea of ministry entirely, in some cases even abandoning the faith. I have often thought that young Samuel was broken into ministry in an extraordinary manner. He saw his mentor Eli's imperfections *after* God had become so real to him. That perhaps is what saved him.

A CLOSE RELATIONSHIP
WITH GOD

Looking back on my life, it is almost certainly what saved me from giving up. When I was in my first pastorate in Palmer, Tennessee, when I was nineteen, God graciously revealed Himself to me in unusual power—showing me how real Jesus is, how true the Bible is. I am humbled that God would deal with me in that manner. It set me up for things coming down the road that almost certainly would have destroyed me, including not only seeing hypocrisy in leadership but also having to face liberal teaching (that denied the infallibility of Scripture) years later. I was even given visions

(I never had them before) that supernaturally warned me of certain leaders I had hero-worshiped.

God spoke directly to Samuel so powerfully that the young man could never doubt God's existence and sovereignty. Samuel, having heard God speak, dutifully ran to Eli to see what he wanted (1 Sam. 3:5). Eli knew nothing and told him to go back to bed. After the third occasion Eli realized something unusual was happening and told Samuel to reply to God, "Speak, for your servant is listening" (v. 10). The next day Eli forced the young Samuel to reveal what was going on: "May God deal with you, be it ever so severely, if you hide from me anything he told you" (v. 17). Samuel then had to tell Eli that God was going to judge Eli himself and his family, a scary word for anybody to have to relate, not to mention one so young. But to Eli's credit, he replied, "He is the Lord; let him do what is good in his eyes" (v. 18). Samuel then grew up under Eli's supervision therefore with no illusion about his mentor. It was, however, a great mercy that Samuel discovered for himself how real God was; otherwise, the whole situation—with the wickedness that Eli was overlooking—could have destroyed him.

It is very, very important that a person going into Christian ministry has a solid relationship with God and also a sound doctrine of sin and knowledge of the human heart. "The heart is deceitful above all things," said Jeremiah. "Who can understand it?" (Jer. 17:9). If we have a naïve view of people, we are an easy target for the devil to bring down. It is said of Jesus: "He did not need man's testimony about man, for he knew what was in a man" (John 2:25). The subsequent failures of Judas Iscariot and Simon Peter therefore did not take Jesus by surprise.

WE ARE ALL CALLED INTO MINISTRY

This caution applies to any reader of this book. You may not be called into what we call full-time Christian ministry, but you are absolutely called to develop a solid relationship with God. It is not only to those in public ministry that God reveals Himself to, but He also does this with all those who want a close relationship with Him. *You are called to ministry.* Your calling to be a nurse, secretary, physician, salesperson, accountant, housewife, lawyer, or truck driver is just as important as being the next Billy Graham. The question is, do you want a close relationship with God? I hope you want this. James said, "Come near to God and he will come near to you" (James 4:8). God loves to surprise the person who feels the most unworthy, the most insignificant, and the most unlikely—if they desire to know God intimately. If you have such a desire, congratulations! That desire was put there by God. He would not give you that desire if He did not have further plans for you.

James said, "Not many of you should presume to be teachers, my brothers, because you know that we who teach will be judged more strictly" (James 3:1). I soon began to realize after beginning my ministry that people set me apart and looked up to me. I never—ever—felt worthy of this. I know too much about myself to take their adulation seriously.

And so too in writing this book. I do not want to mislead you or promise you more than can be delivered. Neither do I want to send you on a guilt trip because you cannot totally forgive God for the things He has allowed in your life. As I said, we all are what we are by the grace of God and can only do what we are called to do by the same grace of God. As St. Augustine (354–430) put it, "Give what Thou commandest and command what Thou wilt."[1] Or as Charles Wesley (1707–1788) put it in one of his hymns, "All my help from Thee I bring."[2] If we are able to come through with what God asks of us, it will be by His help alone. I do come to you with a sincere conviction that I am supposed to write this book, even with the title that some people could misunderstand at first.

God cares how you feel. Your feelings matter to Him very much indeed. Jesus never forgot what it was like when He was on this earth, being tempted at all points as we are but without sin. For this reason He is to this very day touched with the feeling of our weaknesses (Heb. 4:15). He doesn't moralize us, scold us, or make us feel substandard because we have a particular weakness. If you have been disillusioned that He the Creator God, with whom the buck stops and who controls all events, allowed you to suffer as you have, I want to say right now that I don't blame you. God could have stopped what happened but didn't. You are therefore very, very hurt and possibly very, very angry.

THREE REASONS WHY YOU SHOULD TOTALLY FORGIVE GOD

At the same time I shall be bold and let you know up front that I hope to lead you gently but definitely to the place that you will eventually and totally let God off the hook for allowing what He did.

Why? First because of *what it will do for you*. I can safely promise you an inner freedom and release you never dreamed possible. We must forgive those on the earth who have hurt us, and we must forgive God in heaven who let things happen that hurt us. In much the same way as we experience this peace when we totally forgive those who have hurt us, so too when you come to the place you let God off the hook. An extraordinary joy in your heart will be yours. As I say in my book *Total Forgiveness*, this is what happens when you let others off the hook—regardless how evil they were or how hurt you continue to be. Don't wait for them to apologize. Chances are they never well. Chances are too that they don't even think they have done anything wrong! Like it or not, most people we have to forgive honestly do not feel they have done the slightest thing wrong! If you wait for them to repent, you could go to your grave in bitterness.

Moreover, *don't go to them* and tell them how hurt you are. This forgiveness should happen in your *heart*. I myself have had to forgive a lot of people over the years. Never once did I say a word to them (unless they *asked* me to). It would have been counterproductive had I done so. I have had more than one occasion to be in the presence of someone I had to forgive in my heart, but they (hopefully) did not have a clue I had been hurt by them. I sought not to tell anybody what they did. I tried to put them at ease if I were in their company. I made it a point, if the opportunity presented itself, not to let them feel the slightest guilt. I did my best to make it easy for them to save face. And the biggest thing of all: I prayed for them—never telling them that of course. Daily. Sincerely. I don't merely say, "God, I commit them to you." No. God doesn't like that! *I ask God to bless them.* And I must mean it. And guess what? The peace that comes from doing this is far greater than the bitterness one had before. When you see the benefit of total forgiveness, it almost seems like a selfish matter to forgive them!

So I say to you as lovingly and sincerely as I know how: forgive them. Totally. And the greater the evil they did, the greater blessing to you—if you forgive them! The greater the suffering, the greater the anointing and blessing that come from the Holy Spirit. So with forgiving others totally—no matter what they did to you.

My point is: I hope you will come to the place you can do this with God. I will return to this below, showing you further how to do this. Totally forgiving God means you set Him free, let Him off the hook, and affirm Him even though He let some horrible things happen to you. Your life will be changed; you will never be the same again.

Second, I ask you to forgive God also because of what it will do for Him. If you have a desire to please God—and I pray this is the case with you—you are now presented with an opportunity on a silver platter to please Him instantly. It will please Him to no end that you are able totally to let Him off the hook. He only wants what is best for you. He knows better than anyone what it will do for you if you do this.

However, totally forgiving God will not mean relief for Him, as if He will say, "Oh, I am so glad they did this. I feel bad for what I did, and now I am set free." I'm afraid it won't be like that, as we will see further below. But if you are able to forgive Him at this stage—before reading any further, you will please Him. This is because God will rejoice in the freedom you find. As I said, God only wants what is best for us. Were you to forgive Him—the sooner the better—He rejoices in what it will mean for you, including an absence of bitterness that has been so draining on your whole personality. The bitterness you and I feel over our hurt toward God eats away at our souls, our emotional state, our minds, even affecting our relationships with people—not just our relationships with God. In any case, you will please and honor God once you let Him off the hook, set Him free. And never look back once you have done this.

God Will Vindicate Himself One Day

Third, you should totally forgive God because of how you will feel on that final day coming down the road when *God clears His name.* This is something He will do. He looks forward to doing it. God the Father is the most maligned person in the universe He made, and He will delight in clearing His name. Moreover, He will do it perfectly. Convincingly. Before all people who ever lived. Before the angels. Before the devil and all the evil powers.

You may ask: If He so looks forward to it, why doesn't He do it now? I don't know. But as we have to wait, so does He, for some reason, choose to wait for the appointed time.

How will He do it? I have no idea. But when I consider how He vindicates below, this being what He does so brilliantly, it is just a bare hint how He will do it when He openly and finally clears His name. Vindicating His servants is what God does best. He *loves* doing it. The key: don't help Him. He delights to do it all by Himself. Thank you! And He will do it in a way you would never have imagined.

Take Mordecai the Jew in the Old Testament. Mordecai was a close relative to Queen Esther. Through Mordecai's care and shrewdness, Esther was chosen to be the new queen in ancient Babylon. Mordecai, however, did some extremely daring things; some of them seemed utterly unwise. What he did made no sense at all. But God not only eventually cleared Mordecai, vindicating him openly, but also punished Haman the hateful enemy of Mordecai before all the people (Esther 3–7). Nobody would have remotely dreamed of Mordecai being cleared, much less could they have come up with the way it was done. It is one of the most thrilling and glorious stories in the Old Testament.

What God delights in doing with His people—whether it be Abraham, Jacob, Joseph, Moses, or Mordecai—He will one day do for Himself. What God does and doesn't do at times makes no sense at all. But one day He will vindicate Himself. I can't wait. I will be there. You will be there. It will be the day of days, an Omega point toward which all history is moving.

My point is this. How wonderful it will be if we are among those who cleared God's name in advance of that day. I want to be on the winning side now! All men and all women will bend the knee on that day to proclaim Jesus Christ as Lord (Phil. 2:9–11). Those who do it now will participate in God's own vindication then—and love every minute of it.

How will He do it? I have no idea. But as the great missionary to Africa David Livingstone put it, "I do not know how the great loving Father will bring out light at last, but He knows, and He will do it."[3]

CHAPTER TWO

Habakkuk's Complaints

How long, O LORD, must I call for help, but you do not listen? Or cry out to you, "Violence!" but you do not save? Why do you make me look at injustice? Why do you tolerate wrong?

—HABAKKUK 1:2–3

If God both can and wants to abolish evil, then how come evil's in the world?

—EPICURUS (342–270 B.C.)

I HAVE TRIED TO envision who might be reading these lines. Perhaps you have just learned you have cancer. Maybe your closest friend or loved one has been snatched from you. You have been the victim of an evil conspiracy and have no way of defending yourself. You were raped. An authority figure took advantage of you and molested you. You found out your spouse has been unfaithful to you. You have been falsely accused. You realize you married the wrong person and you are stuck. A tornado ripped through your house and destroyed everything at the very time you sought to get closer to God. You have lost your job. Your home. Your savings. Your spouse has left you. Your best friend betrayed you. God let this happen.

There were many questions put to me over the years, ones I especially remember from my twenty-five years of pastoral and preaching ministry in Westminster Chapel. The question that topped the list—and which was the most difficult to answer—was: Why can't I find a husband/wife? Never did I feel so helpless as when a man or woman came to see me and eventually admitted what was their deepest hurt or concern. I never had a good answer. Other questions were: What happens to people after they die who have never heard the gospel? The question asked most often when I talked to people in the streets when giving out tracts was: If there truly is a God, why does He allow evil and suffering?

Parts of this chapter may seem like I am being too much like a preacher or theologian. I realize that theological or philosophical issues don't intrigue everybody, and some readers may want to read past part of the material in this chapter quickly. But I would not be doing my job if I avoided the *very* sort of issue that bedevils some people.

Two Worldviews

There are two theological worldviews that are polar opposites: theodicy and existentialism. *Theodicy* refers to the governing and purposeful ways of God, that there is order and reason for our being in the universe. At the other end is *existentialism*, the view that there is no purpose in the universe—that we are thrown into our existence; we will never know why we are here. The historic Christian position is that there is indeed purpose in the world God made and that one day this will be made clear. Existentialism offers no hope that we will ever understand why we are here.

Many years ago I spent an afternoon with one of my professors at Trevecca Nazarene University in Nashville, Tennessee, Dr. A. K. Bracken. He said to me as I was leaving, "Now let me ask you a question. Why did God create the world knowing that man would suffer?" I could not answer the question then—or now. It is the most ancient and most difficult of all theological questions. It is also the chief question some people use to allow them, with a degree of assurance, to reject the notion of God. Epicurus's question—If God both can and wants to abolish evil, then how come evil's in the world?—invites the conclusion for some that God does not exist. And yet His question need not lead to that conclusion; it may also lead to faith. In any case it is a basis for discussion. After all, if God does exist, one should surely want to explore the question, why does God allow suffering? God Himself is not upset by this question.

Two Choices

I would say we all have basically two choices in the light of the question of evil and suffering: (1) to conclude there is no God, or (2) *ask God Himself* why He allows suffering. He might, after all, reply to you. Habakkuk's complaint that God does not listen was later overruled by God's promise to show up.

One person after another has said to me over the years, "I am an atheist." I sometimes reply, "You have great faith." What! Faith to be an atheist? Yes. Absolutely! The atheist is choosing to believe there is no God. He or she must actually exercise faith that there is no God. "What may be known about God is plain to them, because God has made it plain to them," says Paul (Rom. 1:19). The atheist is a person therefore who has made a choice to reject what God knows is plain to him or her. Believing that there is no God, then, is the consequence of a choice he or she makes. That choice is often made upon the premise that if God existed, He would not allow suffering. Since there is suffering and evil in this world, some people conclude there is no God. They, quite understandably, reason that a loving, powerful God would surely stop suffering. But He obviously doesn't stop it—at least He hasn't stopped it as you are now reading this book. He will, however, stop it one day; He promised that a time would come when *there would be no more death, crying, or pain* (Rev. 21:4). But that time is future. Death exists now. Crying exists now. Pain exists now. This to some proves that God does not exist.

THE EXAMPLE OF JESUS

Anticipating the day when injustice will be finally abolished, King David in writing Psalm 8 rejoiced prophetically that God has put everything under man's feet! Man is crowned with glory and honor. God has consequently put *everything* under his feet (vv. 5–6). "Really? You could have fooled me!" one might say. It hardly appears today that man is crowned with glory with everything under his feet. It looks more like man, instead of being on top, is totally *under* the weight of evil, prejudice, unkindness, terror, apparent random in nature, a God who has no control over creation, hate, and injustice! But the psalmist is speaking prophetically— referring not only to the future day of days but to the death, resurrection, ascension, and second coming of God's Son, Jesus Christ. The writer of Hebrews, referring to Psalm 8, affirms David's word to the hilt and even says that God left *nothing* that is not subject to man (Heb. 2:8). Again we may say, "Really? Surely not!"

But the writer of Hebrews writes not only prophetically but then states the obvious: "Yet at present *we do not see* everything subject to him" (Heb. 2:8, emphasis added). Quite. Evil reigns. Suffering continues. Injustice thrives. We certainly do not *see* evil under our feet. Yet. But what *do* we see? "*We see Jesus*, who was made a little lower than the angels, now crowned with glory and honor because he suffered death, so that by the grace of God he might taste death for everyone" (v. 9, emphasis added).

The day of which I spoke in the previous chapter is future. So what do we see *now*? We see Jesus. He is the mirror of things to come. And He is our example in the meantime.

The Bible categorically affirms that on that day there will be an end to evil, injustice, pain, and suffering. That is the firm, unwavering position of the Word of God. Believing this therefore is to affirm God's integrity, and it also means we may choose to let Him off the hook for the evil in the world in the meantime. That means totally forgiving God for all He has allowed. As we saw above, one day God will clear His name. All of us, however, are invited to do it now— believing His Word without having to wait for the day He does it openly.

The Bible: God's Integrity

The Bible is God's integrity put on the line. By believing His Word, we know in advance of the final day that we will not be disappointed.

You may ask: What is the evidence for this?

I reply: God's integrity.

You may say: That is not good enough for me.

I reply: I truly understand how you feel.

You may say: Then convince me that the Bible is true.

I reply: I wish I could.

You may say: Please try.

I reply: There are only two ways (that I know of) by which one comes to see that the Bible is true: (1) the external witness (for example, archeology, testimonies of people, the survival of the Jews) and (2) the internal witness (the testimony of the Holy Spirit).

To prefer to be convinced by the external witness will end up in endless investigation, which could go on for years without any satisfaction. The internal witness of the Holy Spirit is totally satisfying and comes as one comes to Christ in faith, then pursuing Him and being persistent in faith. If you will be humbly open to reading the Bible with the view of asking the Holy Spirit to help you understand it, you are likely to feel convicted of your sins, which only the Holy Spirit can achieve in a person. The same Holy Spirit will lead you to Jesus Christ, who died for our sins. Although you may not be ready yet, I pray you will eventually reach the place that you will sincerely pray:

> *Lord Jesus Christ, I need You. I want You. I know I am a sinner. I am sorry for my sins. Forgive my sins. Wash my sins by Your blood. I welcome Your Holy Spirit into my heart. As best as I know how, I give You my life. Amen.*

If you prayed this prayer, read on. God will never leave you or forsake you (Heb. 13:5). Jesus promised that He would be with us always—to the end (Matt. 28:20). You will also have the Holy Spirit who, I believe, will make this book clearer than ever.

JESUS THE FORERUNNER

Jesus is the forerunner of what may be true of all of us. Have you experienced suffering and thought that God took no notice of it? *Nobody experienced suffering and injustice as Jesus did.* But He opened not His mouth throughout the greatest pain and unfairness any person in the world ever suffered (Isa. 53:7). He did not complain to God His Father. He did not explain Himself to His critics. The greatest freedom is having nothing to prove, and Jesus had total freedom. Consider how He was hated. Consider the unfairness of His trial. Consider how He suffered. God sent His eternal Son into the world to become flesh—just like us—to demonstrate that *He fully knows what we are feeling.* He was tried, tested, and tempted at all points like we are but without sin (Heb. 4:15). He endured the cross and hated its shame and stigma. But He was raised from the dead and is now sitting at God's right hand.

Yes indeed, one day God will clear His name. We can therefore take Psalm 8 and Hebrews 2:7–9 to the bank, for as surely as Jesus suffered and was raised from the dead, so will you and I be raised to experience His open vindication before every person who ever lived.

RUNNING FROM THINKING

If you are an atheist but are still reading this book, may I address you in particular? I would put another suggestion: to conclude there is no God can sometimes be running from the challenge to think more deeply about it. For one thing, most people who have told me that they don't believe the Bible haven't read it! So too is it easy to dismiss the existence of God and His integrity in one stroke merely if your main premise for disbelief is that an omnipotent and loving God would surely not allow suffering. With respect, that does not always require a lot of thinking. But to follow through with a robust belief in God's utter purity and justice is a huge challenge! It will set our minds to work. God gave us minds. The Christian faith was designed partly to teach us how to think. Asking hard questions and pursuing answers also shows—in part—that we care enough *to try* to get to the bottom of the matter.

The question *Why does God allow suffering?* relates to the problem of evil in philosophy. There are perhaps three answers to this question: one is to say there is no such God; another is to say we do not know; the other is an equally honest reply: *that we might believe.* Perhaps you have never considered that a reason God allows suffering is that you might have faith. That at first may seem to be the most preposterous notion you ever heard. But bear with me. Read on, for this is one of the main points of this book I will elaborate on. It is in any case the most natural and predictable question in the world people come up with—Why does God allow suffering?—whether they be philosophers, highly learned, or uneducated.

APOLOGIZING FOR GOD?

In the ancient church there arose certain people who became known as apologists, a word taken from the Greek *apologia*—speaking in defense. Apologetics is not apologizing for God—as if to say sorry—but is that branch of theology that attempts to present a rational, intellectual defense of the

Christian faith. It is debatable how much real good apologetics has done for evangelism and the church. Dr. Martyn Lloyd-Jones used to suggest that the rise of Christian apologists of the second century was a sad turn of events, that they did more harm than good in the early church. This is partly because apologetics often seemed to be more concerned with defending the faith against criticisms and objections than aggressively preaching the gospel to the lost. Apologetics can sometimes have a deadening effect on the church. It often thrives on intellectual arguments and cerebral preoccupation rather than experiencing the power of the gospel and the Holy Spirit. It often fails to bring life to the church. It may sometimes help in removing objections people have to the Christian faith, but only the gospel converts people through the power of the Holy Spirit. As Samuel Butler (1612–1680) said, "He that complies against his will is of his own opinion still."[1]

PROOFS OF GOD

In the Middle Ages there were theologians who wrote volumes on proofs of God. Anselm (1033–1109) came up with the ontological proof of God that there exists in our minds an idea of a being than which no greater can be conceived; that being does exist and is God. Thomas Aquinas (1224–1274) espoused the cosmological proof of God (Greek *cosmos*, creation or world) that God is the First Cause, the Unmoved Mover in the universe. There followed the teleological proof of God (Greek *telos*, end), argument from design. The existence of order and direction in nature shows purpose in the universe.

The problem with the proofs of God is that the medieval theologians were largely preaching to the choir, as we might say today. In other words, the proofs of God prove God's existence when you believe in Him anyway. These arguments merely confirmed or strengthened one's faith that was already present.

My book, however, is not chiefly about apologetics—as if I needed to defend the existence of God or the truth of the Bible. "Defend the Bible?" asked Charles H. Spurgeon (1834–1892), "I would as soon defend a lion."[2] However, the underlying rationale for this book is to make the case that God is *all that He says He is* in the Bible.

Four Reasons for This Book

Apologetics has a limited role to play in Christian thinking. I myself am not greatly attracted to apologetics, to be honest. I certainly do not write this book in an attempt to prove that God exists. The Bible itself doesn't even do that, so why should I? I write as I do, however—even if it borders on apologetics—for four reasons:

1. To affirm God's integrity

2. To help you see that God has His own reasons for not answering all the questions we want answered

3. To lead you away from any bitterness you may have toward God

4. To help you let Him *totally* off the hook for what He has allowed to happen to you

If one chooses to be an atheist, the issue of forgiving God is of course out of the question; there is no God to forgive. But given the premise that God exists and that He is all-powerful and full of mercy—but who still allows evil—one has a choice between being angry with such a God or affirming Him to be as He is described in the Bible. The God of the Bible is just, pure, faultless, incapable of lying, and full of mercy.

GOD ONLY WANTS WHAT IS BEST FOR US

Perhaps the main point I wish to make in this book is that God does not answer all our questions for our own good. He cares indeed about our feelings. He only wants what is best for us. Believe it or not, He has definite and encouraging reasons for not answering all our prayers. Not only that, but He also delays answering some of our prayers to *make room for faith.*

I therefore write this book to help increase your faith. If all your questions were answered, you would no longer need faith. My heart goes out to you if you struggle to believe. I am going to do my best to encourage you. If I can be an instrument to help increase your faith, I will be thrilled to no end. Faith is what pleases God. "Without faith it is impossible to please God, because anyone who comes to him must believe that he exists *and* that he *rewards* those who earnestly seek him" (Heb. 11:6, emphasis added). I guarantee that you will experience exactly this *reward* if you will not give up.

I now turn to the Old Testament prophet who addressed the ancient problem of evil. He writes as a very normal human being. Perhaps you can identify with his complaints. Habakkuk had basically four complaints, which he directed to God Himself.

HABAKKUK'S INITIAL COMPLAINTS

1. Unanswered prayer

The ancient prophet's initial complaint was that *God does not listen*: "How long, O LORD, must I call for help, but you do not listen?" (Hab. 1:2). The Hebrew word that is translated "listen" is *shema*—a word that means to hear or to obey. If God hears in the Hebraic sense, it means He will *obey our request*. In other words, if He *hears* us, He will answer us. Habakkuk shows that God can, simply, *choose not to hear us*.

And yet Habakkuk's dilemma is not isolated. How often does the psalmist wrestle with the same thing? "Why, O LORD, do you stand far off? Why do you hide yourself in times of trouble?" (Ps. 10:1). "How long, O LORD? Will you forget me forever? How long will you hide your face from me?" (Ps. 13:1). "I cried out to God for help; I cried out to God to hear me.... Will the Lord reject forever?... Has his unfailing love vanished forever? Has his promise failed for all time? Has God forgotten to be merciful?" (Ps. 77:1, 7–9). In the book that bears His name, then, Habakkuk's very first word is a prayer complaining that God does not listen.

It is an eternal principle that any request that is prayed in the will of God will be answered. "This is the confidence we have in approaching God: that if we ask anything according to his will, he hears us" (1 John 5:14). So had Habakkuk not been praying in the will of God? After all, sometimes God's refusal to listen is owing to our willful disobedience. "If you had responded to my rebuke, I would have poured out my heart to you and made my thoughts known to you. But since you rejected me when I called... I will mock when calamity overtakes you.... Then they will call to me but I will not answer" (Prov. 1:23–24, 26, 28). So had Habakkuk been disobedient? No. Habakkuk was interceding for Israel, God's people, and was no doubt caught in the cross fire between Israel's disobedience and God venting His anger on them. Habakkuk's comment, "You do not listen," referred to the way God seemed to be hiding His face from His people.

A natural response toward God when He does not answer our request is often to accuse Him of being uncaring and directly responsible for our hurt. For example, when Mary and Martha sent word to Jesus that their brother—His friend Lazarus—was deathly ill, they were sure Jesus would come to Bethany like a shot to heal Lazarus. But Lazarus died. Jesus showed up four days after the funeral. Both Martha and Mary wanted to accuse Jesus for not coming when they sent for Him: "Lord, if you had been here, my brother would not have died" (John 11:21, 32).

And yet God is always motivating us to pray and seek His face with the promise that He will respond. For example, the words "Call to me and I will answer you" (Jer. 33:3) may set us to praying for a good while. But when God doesn't answer in what we judge to be a reasonable length of time, we may feel let down or sometimes betrayed. The conclusion follows for some: "He must not be there at all. Why should I believe Him when He invites me to call on Him but does not answer?"

That reasoning of course is from our subjective perspective—the way it seems from our point of view. Are we then to set God free from any responsibility for not answering our prayers, and should we totally forgive Him? Yes.

2. God looking the other way during violence

Habakkuk's second complaint is that *God does not see what is happening.* "[I] cry out to you, 'Violence!' but you do not save?" (Hab. 1:2). "'Help! Murder!' I cry, but no one comes to save" (TLB). This seems from our subjective perspective to be the consummate example of God betraying us. When I am seeking God's face and am right in the middle of violence, murder, rape, war, torture—and God turns His head away and seems to look in another direction, what am I to believe? Why should I believe He is there? Why should I believe He cares? Those are the most natural questions in the world.

After the ark of God was returned to Israel by the Philistines, seventy of the people of Beth Shemesh were instantly put to death—merely because they looked into the ark of the Lord (1 Sam. 6:19). Is that fair?

Years later when David had the noble ambition to bring the ark to Jerusalem, a man named Uzzah reached out to steady the ark as it was being carried on a cart and was instantly put to death (2 Sam. 6:6–7). These things happened when the loftiest motives of the people of God were in play. They were attempting to glorify God by bringing the ark of the covenant to a place of honor. Why did this happen? Does this make sense?

There are countless illustrations of people suffering violence, even when they are earnestly attempting to do the will of God—missionaries in various parts of the world who are tortured, young Christians who rededicate their lives to Christ who are murdered, or restored backsliders who come back to the Lord who suddenly experience financial reverse or a fatal illness. Instead of God rewarding them, the thanks some get is to suffer the most shameful kind of violence. I have had people in my vestry sobbing their hearts out who were raped on their way to church, mugged on their way to a prayer meeting, or accosted during a time they were renewing their commitment to God. Who can explain why God would allow violent men to interrupt a church service in Texas and start gunning down people right, left, and center? Or when He lets evil people murder worshipers in Northern Ireland during a Sunday evening service as they are singing hymns to God? Was there a perfectly right reason that God allowed this?

From our perspective it makes no sense. And yet are we to let God off the hook for all this? Yes.

3. Having to endure injustice

Habakkuk's third complaint is that *God does not care.* "Why do you make me look at injustice?" (Hab. 1:3). "Wherever I look I see oppression and bribery and men who love to argue and to fight. The law is not enforced, and there is no justice given in the courts, for the wicked far outnumber the righteous, and bribes and trickery prevail" (TLB). One of the most painful things many have to face is to see injustice carried out in the courts—like one getting away with murder.

The whole of America, rightly or wrongly, will probably be indignant for a long time over two trials of the century in recent years: one of a famous football player accused of murdering his wife; the other of an apparently careless mother for allegedly killing her child. Both were acquitted. This is to say nothing of countless verdicts in courts where evil clearly won the day. There are a vast number of crimes—of rape, murder, theft, torture, lying—that never get reported in newspapers or on television. Most cases never get enough profile in the media for people to take notice. When judges are bribed or juries are prejudiced, what are the innocent to do? Whereas some world leaders such as Adolf Hitler and dictators such as Saddam Hussein are found out, most are not. Think of the people who suffered at their hands. When one reads of the accounts of six million Jews in the Holocaust or of black people being slaughtered during the apartheid days in South Africa, we ask, "Where was God in all this?" Are we to clear God's name in the light of this? Yes.

4. God's tolerance of evil

Habakkuk's fourth complaint was that of God *knowingly permitting evil to thrive.* "Why do you tolerate wrong?" (Hab. 1:3). Habakkuk acknowledges that the buck stops with God. God Himself *tolerated* wrong. He could have stopped it but allowed it to go on instead. God is all-powerful. He could stop all the aforementioned suffering and injustice immediately. But He doesn't. Why? The prophet Habakkuk therefore addressed the question *to God Himself*: Why do you tolerate wrong? What is more, says Habakkuk, "the law is paralyzed"—no one in Judah seems to give it respect, and God is apparently doing nothing about it (v. 4). Evil and decadence galore prevail throughout Judah. Nobody cares. "God, You don't even seem to care. Don't *You* realize that Your own Word is being treated with contempt?" "Wicked hem in the righteous so that justice is perverted" (v. 4). So what's going on?

By the way, do you envy Habakkuk for getting to talk to God as he did? If *you* had a chance to tell God a thing or two, what would you say to Him?

It is perhaps surprising that this question—Why do you tolerate wrong?—does not come up in the Bible more than it does. God is not offended by it. He is not threatened by it. And yet there are times when we are driven to our knees with tears and agony to ask why. There are awful things going on all over the world—famine, racial injustice, greed, corruption in governments, war, unspeakable pain, theft, incurable diseases, and hurricanes showing up where it is least deserved, as in poverty-stricken Haiti—so we ask why.

What I myself have personally experienced in the way of disappointment in my lifetime is virtually nothing compared to what is existent all over the world. And yet I still ask a question that I asked for weeks and months after my mother's death (she was only forty-three) in 1953: Why? In those days someone gave me a recording of a song sung by a Southern Gospel quartet called "We'll Talk It Over," which I listened to for hours and hours for weeks and weeks. The words assured me that, bye and bye, I would be able to ask God the reasons why and He would then give me answers.

Joni Eareckson Tada has become a household name in the evangelical world. As a teenager she was severely injured in a diving accident that left her a quadriplegic. She refused to blame God but chose to bless Him instead. After she spoke at Westminster Chapel on one occasion, she said to me, "I love being here. It is the theology that has been preached here that gave me a sense of sanity and reason to live after my accident." She specifically referred to the teaching of the sovereignty of God and mentioned Martyn Lloyd-Jones and the writings of A. W. Pink. She does not pretend to understand why God allowed this. One of her favorite songs (on her website) contains these words:

> Someday He'll make it plain to me,
> Someday when I His face shall see;
> Someday from tears I shall be free,
> For someday I shall understand.[3]
>
> —LYDIA S. LEECH (1842–1870)

CHAPTER THREE

Let Down

By faith Abraham, when called to go to a place he would later receive as his inheritance, obeyed and went... [and yet God] gave him no inheritance here, not even a foot of ground.

—Hebrews 11:8; Acts 7:5

Where is that inheritance for which he hoped? It must surely have occurred to him that he had been deceived by God.... It was the outstanding virtue of Abraham that he withstood this temptation bravely, a fact which comes from faith alone.

—John Calvin (1509–1564)

T HE ORIGIN OF the idea of breaking the betrayal barrier, found in Dr. James Dobson's book *When God Doesn't Make Sense*, lies in the passages above. I will never forget where I was when I was hugely gripped by Acts 7:5 over thirty years ago. It gave me an entirely new perspective on how God deals with those whom He has sovereignly called to service. Both Acts 7:5 and Hebrews 11:8 state clearly that the land of Canaan was to be Abraham's inheritance, or possession. That place was Canaan. But according to Acts 7:5 Abraham *did not get it*, not even a foot of ground. The irony of Abraham's experience, not to mention all those people of faith described in Hebrews 11, is that he and they didn't give up; they "were all commended for their faith, yet *none of them received what had been promised*" (Heb. 11:39, emphasis added).

What! They did not receive what *God* promised them? That is what it says.

Those stalwarts of faith in Hebrews 11 had at least two things in common. First, not a single one of them had the privilege of repeating what had been done previously; they all were required to do something new and different. Enoch walked with God and was taken to heaven (Heb. 11:5). Noah walked with God but was not taken to heaven; he was commanded to build an ark (v. 7). That was a feat never done before—or since. Abraham walked with God and was neither taken to heaven nor required to build an ark. He simply started walking and did not know where he was going (v. 8). So goes the list of these people—of whom the world was not worthy (v. 38). Second, each one of them had in common that they broke the betrayal barrier, which I will now explain.

BETRAYED BY GOD?

God does not betray us—ever. It has never happened. It never will happen. But for some of us our *perception* is that we are betrayed. In other words, some of us *feel* betrayed. We can amass our reasons for this feeling and thereby feel totally convinced we have been betrayed. And yet it is only our subjective perception that is in play, although it is difficult to see this at the time—or for a long time.

Perhaps not every follower of Jesus has felt a time of being betrayed by the Lord. I once reckoned that the overwhelming majority of Christians have felt this. Over the last fifteen years, having discussed this with trusted friends, I have been forced to reassess this opinion. I wondered too if only those called to do a special work for God sooner or later—even if for a while—feel betrayed by Him. I even once surmised that ten out of ten such men and women feel that. I believe I made the mistake of assuming that what I myself have felt is what others felt as well. So I have climbed down from my previous point of view on this.

Not only that, but perhaps *betrayed* is not the exact feeling that all experience. I have had sincere Christians say candidly to me that they never even *felt* betrayed by God. While part of me wants to say to them, "Be careful; you're not home yet," I recognize the sovereignty of God in this matter. For example, Jesus told Peter, "'When you are old you will stretch out your hands, and someone else will dress you and lead you where you do not want to go.' Jesus said this to indicate the kind of death by which Peter would glorify God." (John 21:18). Peter immediately asked Jesus, "Lord, what about him?"—meaning John. Jesus replied: "If I want him to remain alive until I return, what is that to you? You must follow me" (vv. 21–22). In a word: whereas Peter was required to die a martyr's death, John lived to old age, well into his nineties. Both were equally sovereign vessels of God, both equally loved by God, but they were not required to suffer equally.

And yet some Christians do feel betrayed by God. To say what percentage experiences this would be to indulge in unprofitable speculation. I only know what I myself have felt. It must have been how Abraham felt, having been promised the land of Canaan but did not get even a foot of ground. Rightly or wrongly, deceived is the word John Calvin used. Perhaps *disappointed* is a better word. Or, simply, let down. I do know, however, that Jeremiah said, "O LORD, you deceived me, and I was deceived" (Jer. 20:7).

I think also there are at least two ways of understanding this feeling of betrayal. One example is when a trusted friend betrays you—and you equate this hurt with *God* having done it. I know what it is to have a mentor who I felt had been given to me sovereignly by God—and have that same friend throw me under the bus, as they say. This happened to me many years ago, long before we went to England. Why did God lead me to believe this friend was one I could trust? Or was it God who led me to think this? Was it my own immaturity or lack of judgment? In any case, when this person utterly abandoned me in my time of deepest need, I was overwhelmed with grief. Some think I had an emotional breakdown. Although I do believe I have totally forgiven this person, the trauma of that era left a scar on my psyche that has stayed with me to this day.

The second way to understand the sense of divine betrayal is what I will discuss below. It is when I was absolutely certain I had heard from God—and can only conclude that, if I did, I was surely betrayed. And yet I do not believe I was betrayed.

I repeat: God never betrays us. But we may *feel* betrayed. I do not believe He ever deserts us; we only *feel* deserted. I do not believe God truly lets us down; we only *feel* let down.

VISIONS

Many years ago, while I was a pastor in Palmer, Tennessee, and attending Trevecca Nazarene University, I began to have visions. These visions—a dozen or more—came passively and unexpectedly during a period that lasted roughly six months, beginning in late 1955, shortly after the occasion God dealt with me so graciously when Jesus Christ was made so real to me. One of my first visions was that of my dad sitting on the front row of a large tent in which I was doing the preaching. He was wearing a brown pinstripe suit. He was smiling and clearly approving of my ministry. This greatly encouraged me, as I feared he would be unhappy with my recent theological change not to mention a different denominational direction that was at hand. He had named me after his favorite preacher—Dr. R. T. Williams, general superintendent in the Church of the Nazarene—and so my dad had great plans for me in that denomination. I knew from that vision, however, he would be happy with me.

But when I returned home from Trevecca in June 1956, having resigned my church in Palmer, he was not only displeased, but he also accused me of breaking with God. This was a shock to me. As it happened that same summer, I was part of a nonstarter called Tri-State Evangelistic Campaign, near my hometown of Ashland, Kentucky. We purchased a huge tent that seated two thousand. I also thought this fit the vision. But my dad never came near that tent meeting, and he continued in his outspoken opposition to my new direction. The tent meeting closed down within a month. We never had more than thirty people or so to attend. It was a total failure and a massive embarrassment to me.

I felt betrayed. I had not asked for that vision. It was so

real to me. I was convinced it was from the Holy Spirit. Could it have been?

There were other visions. One was that of my dad walking down the center aisle in a church that had windows on only one side. He was wearing a light green suit. In the vision he walked down the aisle to the front, turned, and went back. That was the vision. Six years later when I accepted the pastorate of a church in Carlisle, Ohio, I could not help but notice that there were windows on only one side of the church. My dad phoned to say he was coming to hear me preach the following Sunday. I said to my wife, Louise: "He will be wearing a light green suit and will at some point walk down the center aisle to the front, then walk back." When he came to see us, he brought with him a light green suit. The vision was perfectly fulfilled. At one point he walked down the center aisle to the front, then turned back. That was it. The vision was completely and totally fulfilled. Whatever did it mean? But there is more: my ministry in Ohio was rejected by that church, and I returned to Florida in early 1964 with a very uncertain future.

Why was one of the visions perfectly fulfilled and the other not at all?

Another vision came to me in June 1956 as I was returning to Ashland, having just left Trevecca and also my church in Palmer. As I drove in my 1955 Chevrolet (my grandmother's gift), I noticed the dashboard of my car suddenly looked like that of a *1953* Chevrolet. I knew my cars back then, but I wondered why such a strange vision. But one month later my Grandma Kendall took back the new 1955 Chevrolet she had bought for me to use while I was the pastor in Palmer. I now had to get a job. A man who owned a dry cleaning establishment approached me and asked if I would work for him and be his driver. When I got into his car—there it was: the dashboard of a 1953 Chevrolet. That comforted me to no end. I knew God had prepared me for this difficult time.

There were other visions. Some of them were fulfilled; others were not. But one of them clearly indicated that I would have an international ministry.

In my anxiety to please my dad, I assured him that I had not broken with God, that the Lord was going to give me an international ministry. "When?" he asked. "In one year," I guessed. He said, "Will you put that in writing?" "Sure," I confidently replied. I was so convinced that it would happen any day (that was August 1956) that I signed my name to the prediction of my future ministry, which I really believed would happen in a month or two. But a year later I wasn't in the ministry at all. Ten years later I worked as a door-to-door vacuum cleaner salesman (although I did some preaching).

Visions. They all came to me unsought and seemed equally credible. These were not dreams, by the way; they were open visions. If they weren't of God, you could have fooled me! They were absolutely real. And yet some were literally fulfilled; others were not. Why?

I felt betrayed.

But I didn't give up. I could never forget how real the person of Jesus had been to me, how real the Bible became, and how convinced I was of its infallibility and reliability. I am so glad I persisted in faith. I knew there had to be a reason for these visions. I was determined to break through what I call the betrayal barrier.

And yet another odd thing happened to me upon my departure from the church in Ohio over forty-five years ago. I began to have (what I can only call) satanic dreams. They were apparently prophetic. They put me in the deepest bondage; I would wait for something bad to happen to get the fulfillment of the dream behind me, hoping I would never have another. These dreams have persisted for many, many years—I still have them. They are not of God; they must be of the devil. And yet I read: "The one who was born of God keeps him safe, and the *evil one cannot harm him*" (1 John 5:18, emphasis added). Really? My experience (so it seems to me) is a contradiction to that verse in the Bible. I have had continual distress from the devil all these years.

I have therefore felt betrayed that God would let these evil things happen in my dreams in the light of 1 John 5:18. For what it's worth, I have shared this in the past with certain trusted friends—including Dr. Martyn Lloyd-Jones—some of whom felt the need to cast the devil out of me. I accepted their opinion and prayers, but the evil dreams have not left.

Breaking the Betrayal Barrier

Not all who read these lines will identify with the need to do what is outlined in this section. This part of the book is mainly for those who have truly felt a sense of divine betrayal. All others may wish to pass over this section or, possibly, try to sympathize with those who have experienced grief you yourself have not felt.

If *you* are one of those who have felt that God betrayed you or grossly let you down, what next? If this experience fits you, I come now to urge you to achieve the greatest challenge a believer can accept: to break the betrayal barrier. It means not to give up; to keep trusting the same God who promised certain things even though you feel He has not kept His word in some areas. It is persistent faith. There are basically two kinds of faith: saving faith (which makes you a Christian and fits you for heaven) and persistent faith (the faith that achieves what God envisages for you here below). The faith exemplified in those men and women in Hebrews 11 is not saving faith but *persistent* faith.

In the twentieth century the aviation industry achieved a tremendous breakthrough—when an airplane broke the sound barrier, flying faster than the speed of sound. It was a major scientific accomplishment. Breaking the betrayal barrier however is a *spiritual* achievement—perhaps the greatest achievement you or I can carry out. It is accomplished by persistent faith. Few, sadly, seem to achieve it.

I don't mean to be unfair, but my pastoral experience suggests that not very many people actually break the betrayal barrier. A very small number indeed apparently personally experience what the biblical people of faith eventually came to enjoy. Sadly, most never—ever—seem to discover what their inheritance would have been. It is not that they all reject God. Many keep going to church, yes. Some keep busy doing religious things. Some have important positions in the church, often in leadership. But in their hearts, they are dismayed that God let them down. Others simply wander back and forth from the church to the world. Some stop praying and reading their Bibles. Some quit going to church altogether. They get angry, saying sarcastically to God, "Thanks a lot. You let me down big time. I'm out of here." Or something like that.

But not Abraham. Or Isaac. Or Jacob. Or Moses. Or any of those described in Hebrews 11.

What about you? Will you break the betrayal barrier? *You can.*

I used to express the hope that the people at Westminster Chapel would be like those described in Hebrews 11. Why must it be the odd one or two? *Why not all of us?* We are all equally challenged, and we all can do what those people of faith did. It comes by *not giving up*, persisting in faith despite all the odds being against you. If Winston Churchill in World War II could speak to a nation those words that kept all Britain so encouraged—Never, never, never, never give up[1]—why not you and me when God is looking for those who will trust His Word?

I'm sorry, but it isn't easy.

HOW TO BREAK THE BETRAYAL BARRIER

For those readers who identify with a feeling of divine betrayal, I believe this section is for you. How does one break the betrayal barrier? I suggest the following:

1. Know that it is God's idea that you break the betrayal barrier.

It is what He Himself very much wants of you. God often plays hard-to-get. I call it the divine tease. It is said of Hezekiah that the Lord "*left him to test him* and to know everything that was in his heart" (2 Chron. 32:31, emphasis added). It is an irony that God puts obstacles in our way when we are most determined to do His will. Instead of instantly rewarding us, He backs off from us! Like it or not, it is one of God's characteristics that His way of drawing you closer to Him is often to do the very thing that puts you off Him. So many get annoyed and feel rejected when this happens. I therefore suggest to you, the next time things go terribly wrong and God hides His face from you, press on all the more. Don't give up. The breakthrough will come and is worth waiting for.

2. The sense of betrayal by God in truth may well present you with the *greatest opportunity you will ever have* to know Him intimately.

Strange as it may seem, the Lord plays hard-to-get because He loves you so much. He wants to know how much you truly want Him; whether or not you will be rebuffed, put off or angry by His keeping a painful distance from you. Speaking personally, my own utmost desire is to have a greater anointing of the Holy Spirit. Whether this is a spiritual or natural wish, I only know it means more to me than anything. It has been my own personal experience, however, that any increase of anointing I may have had in my seventy-six years has come through great hardship, extreme difficulties, extraordinary hurts, disappointment—and, yes, feeling betrayed by the very One I have sought to please the most.

I do not dismiss the possibility that one's anointing can be increased through various ways: by more prayer, fasting, giving, reading the Bible, or by the laying on of hands of a godly person. But as far as I can tell, whatever anointing I have has come chiefly by my saying, "Yes, Lord," and persisting in faith when confronted with an impossible situation.

3. Don't complain.

This is something that cannot be overemphasized. God hates murmuring, grumbling, and complaining. What is more, it gets us nowhere! It doesn't work if you are trying to get God's attention! And if Christians knew how much God is displeased with grumbling, we would all, almost certainly, stop it! Persistent faith must be laced with gratitude. "Do not be anxious about anything, but in everything, by prayer and petition, *with thanksgiving*, present your requests to God" (Phil. 4:6, emphasis added). Statistics have recently been revealed, as reported by the *Tampa Bay Times*, that thankful people live longer.[2] This finding was not by Christians but by the medical profession. As for Christians, however, I would add: God loves gratitude, and He hates ingratitude. We are commanded to give thanks in all circumstances, not necessarily being thankful for them but *in* them (1 Thess. 5:18). Learn to be thankful and set your heart on replacing grumbling with things you are thankful for. Nothing will change your life like maintaining a spirit of gratitude.

4. Pray more than ever and read your Bible more than ever.

How much do you pray? In my book *Did You Think to Pray?* I actually emphasize *time* you spend with God. Children spell love T-I-M-E. What if God spells love like that? You show your esteem of a person by how much time you give to him or her. By the way, there will be no praying in heaven. In the meantime be assured that God likes your company. Spend time with Him—the more, the better. It is also how you get to know God's *ways*, assuming too that you aspire to know His Word—the Bible. I suggest a Bible reading plan that takes you through the Bible in a year. We should want to know His Word as well as His ways. He esteems His Word above all His name (literal translation of the Hebrew in Psalm 138:2). When you feel let down by God, seek Him in His Word. Spend as much time in the Word as you possibly can—any part of it. Persistent faith is demonstrated by maintaining gratitude alongside consistent prayer. Keep praying; keep reading your Bible. It is how you get to know God and to discover His plan for your life. When you feel let down, pray more than ever. When you feel betrayed, read the Bible more than ever.

5. Walk in the light God gives you.

"If we walk in the light, as he is in the light, we have fellowship with one another, and the blood of Jesus, his Son, purifies us from all sin" (1 John 1:7). If you are faithful in regard to what I have suggested above, here is what you will discover: God will show you things. It is light. Revelation. For example, He will show you *sin* you didn't know you had. He will show you *ways forward* you had not thought about. He will show you *new obedience* that perhaps is long overdue.

In my own life when I vowed to get as close to God as I could—despite feeling betrayed—I began to see my own sins in a surprising and alarming way. My *ingratitude* was brought to my attention. As a consequence I resolved to be a thankful man. My *complaining* suddenly convicted me. So I tried to dignify trials instead of grumbling when they came. My *bitterness* came before me. As a result I sought to be totally forgiving toward all those people who have hurt me. I also felt convicted how little I had talked about the Lord to people I run into all the time—whether on a bus, train, or airplane. It turned me into being a better soulwinner. In any case, persistent faith will be accompanied with a *sense of duty*. When you embrace that sense of duty rather than shrinking back from it, you are on the road to breaking the betrayal barrier.

THE INNER TESTIMONY
OF THE HOLY SPIRIT

The breakthrough I am putting before you is *internal*, not external. You may recall that there are two ways of coming to believe in the inspiration of the Bible: the internal witness and the external witness. So too with breaking the betrayal barrier. The internal witness is the testimony of the Holy Spirit. The external would be that things fall neatly into place and you come to terms with what God has allowed. I am not predicting that things will make sense to you because of an external situation improving. If that happens, good. But that is not what I am suggesting or pointing to here. The inner witness of the Holy Spirit is what I envisage; it is in the heart. It is when God becomes so real to you that you are content with His presence; you are therefore not disillusioned or demoralized because you do not have a logical explanation for things. The internal testimony of the Spirit, then, is what I mean by breakthrough.

I can't predict what it will be like in everyone's situation, but I can testify to what breaking the betrayal barrier has meant to me. In a word: God showed up in a way that was unmistakable. He became absolutely real to me. This has happened more than once. I can only say that when I feel betrayed—which also has happened more than once—and yet I don't give up, God has a way of revealing Himself *never too late, never too early, but always just on time.* The breakthrough leaves me with the feeling I could never truly doubt Him again.

What God has done for me, He will do for you. He is not

a respecter of persons; He does not show favoritism (Acts 10:34). God knows all about you and me. "O LORD, you have searched me and you know me. You know when I sit and when I rise; you perceive my thoughts from afar" (Ps. 139:1–2).

God knows you so well. He knows you backward and forward—your past hurts, present aspirations, feelings, and dilemmas. He remembers details of your past you have forgotten about. He therefore knows *exactly* what will satisfy you. He knows what will comfort you. He knows what will convince you, what will give you peace. That is the way He is and the way He works. You will see in the end—when the light breaks through—that He did not betray you after all. He did not dessert you. Your feeling let down was part of His plan to get your attention.

I pray that *you—if you have felt betrayed by God*—will also experience this internal breakthrough. I would love to think that every reader of this book—if you have felt this betrayal—will be able to testify to this. But not all people do, for some reason. This is why I stated earlier in this chapter that not many experience this breakthrough. Why? My opinion is, they give up too soon. Only a few find it, said Jesus (Matt. 7:14). But it need not be the case with *you*.

God does care how you feel. He knows your frame and mine, remembering always that we are dust (Ps. 103:14). If you need more time and take longer before you can totally forgive God, He is OK about this. He loves you as you are. He will be there waiting for you. He is not rushing you. He will come through for you. I guarantee it. That is, if you persist in faith. Never, never, never, never give up.

PART TWO

God's Perspective

"For my thoughts are not your thoughts, neither are your ways my ways," declares the LORD. "As the heavens are higher than the earth, so are my ways higher than your ways and my thoughts than your thoughts."

—ISAIAH 55:8–9

It ain't those parts of the Bible that I can't understand that bother me, it is the parts that I do understand.

—MARK TWAIN (1835–1910)

CHAPTER FOUR

Why Faith?

Lazarus is dead, and for your sake I am glad I was not there, so that you may believe.

—JOHN 11:14–15

Faith isn't the ability to believe long and far into the misty future. It's simply taking God at His Word and taking the next step.

—JONI EARECKSON TADA

T HERE ARE BASICALLY two ways to understand God, theology, and the Bible. One is to approach these from man's point of view; the other is to approach them from God's point of view. The first part of this book dealt largely with our (man's) point of view. This present section will focus on God's perspective. Sadly, too many people don't bother to think of reading the Bible from God's point of view but only from our subjective perspective. So I invite you to come along with me as we attempt to see things from God's point of view.

How do we know we are trying to understand God from His perspective? Join me now as we look more deeply into the story of Mary, Martha, and Lazarus. Their query and concern ("Please come to Bethany") show their subjective point of view, but Jesus's response ("I'm not coming to Bethany so you can believe") mirrors God's point of view.

Shortly after I began writing this book, someone said to me, "RT, what was the most defining moment of your life?" I had never been asked that before, but I immediately recalled one of my first sermons preached at Westminster Chapel in 1977 on Mary and Martha sending for Jesus. This defining moment actually came not during my preaching but as I read the Scripture—from John 11:14 ("I am glad I was not there, *so that you may believe*"), Jesus's reason for refusing to rush to Bethany to heal Lazarus at the request of Mary and Martha. It was almost certainly the most profound experience I have ever had in the pulpit. It came quite unexpectedly and shaped my thinking forever. I remember telling this to Dr. Martyn Lloyd-Jones a couple days later. I will never forget it; he teared up as I had not seen him do before.

You may recall that I said above that God allows evil and suffering to exist in order *that we might have faith*. I do not say that this is *the* reason God allows evil to exist, but it is certainly part of the explanation. There is no doubt about this. This is because there would be no need for faith if either there were no suffering in this world or God gave the reason regarding suffering to us *now*. It is the presence of evil and the absence of the answer regarding it that allows for the need for faith.

What makes faith *faith* is that we don't have the outward proof or evidence of something but *still believe*. "Now faith is being sure of what we hope for and *certain of what we do not see*" (Heb. 11:1, emphasis added).

THE EMPEROR HAS NO CLOTHES

Christians are sometimes charged with being obscurantists. *Obscurantism* means "deliberately not facing the facts." It means purposeful vagueness or obtuseness, not unlike the proverbial ostrich foolishly sticking his head in the sand, thinking he cannot be seen. I think of certain faith healers you sometimes see on television. They claim people are supernaturally healed because they fall down when prayed for and the audience stands and cheers, believing that healing has taken place. Never mind that so many of these people turn out not to be healed after all; they sometimes will not face the truth that they *haven't* been healed. Mind you, I believe in divine healing. My wife, Louise, was supernaturally healed of a terrible condition more than fifteen years ago. I myself have prayed for people who were truly, literally, and miraculously healed. But sometimes people are *not* healed, yet some live in denial—claiming a miracle when no miracle has taken place. It is a form of obscurantism—not admitting to the obvious but remaining willfully ignorant. He or she does not want to face facts.

The atheist or unbeliever therefore might accuse the Christian of being an obscurantist in the light of the biblical definition of faith: being assured of something without any evidence for it. As believers, then, we may be accused of being obscurantists because we believe in God, the Bible, Jesus's vicarious death on the cross for our sins, His resurrection and ascension to the right hand of God, the Holy Spirit, salvation, the second coming of Jesus, and the final judgment followed by heaven or hell. None of these can be proved.

Take Hans Christian Anderson's (1805–1875) tale about the emperor's new clothes. The emperor was duped into believing that he had beautiful new clothes but which in fact were invisible. His loyal sycophantic followers believed his clothes were glorious. He was paraded naked in public as people cheered the emperor's new clothes. Only a child—being totally honest—openly and bravely spoke the truth, "The emperor doesn't have any clothes on." It broke the spell, and all then admitted to what the child saw.

So are Christians duped into believing that the God of the Bible is all-powerful, loving, faithful, just, and pure? After all, faith is being persuaded of what you don't see! Are we being obscurantists like the emperor's loyal following? The cynic might likewise accuse us Christians of admiring the emperor's new clothes—living in denial because we persist in faith even though God apparently lets us down. We might be accused of being silly, stubborn, or prideful—refusing to admit we have gotten it wrong.

In this book I am urging you to let God off the hook—totally forgiving Him—for what He has permitted that makes no sense to you. But you must remain true to yourself. You forgive Him not because you are unintelligent or are living in a dream world—or are in denial—but because you really do believe His Word.

Let's face it. There are those who hold on to their belief in God merely by culture or tradition and have not given serious inquiry to hard issues such as the problem of evil. We all have seen empty-headed people who say, "I believe the Bible whether it's true or not," "What is to be will be whether it happens or not," or "I believe in the Bible from Genesis to maps" (some Bibles have maps of the Holy Land at the end). Moreover, I have watched people like this crumble overnight when bad things happen to them; their faith dissolves as quickly as the rising sun evaporates the dew on the ground.

A Definition of Faith

A secular person would define faith as *seeing, then believing.* "I will believe it when I see it," the skeptic says. But that is not faith at all according to the Bible. The Bible teaches that faith to be truly *faith* is to believe without seeing. "Faith is being sure of what we hope for and certain of what we do not see" (Heb. 11:1). Yes, being sure and certain and yet having no evidence to prove one got it right. The scoffing mobs said to Jesus when He was hanging on the cross, "Let this Christ, this King of Israel, come down now from the cross, *that we may see and believe*" (Mark 15:32, emphasis added). That, to the secularist, is faith—*seeing, then believing* after you observe the evidence. But faith according to the Bible is to believe without having seen the evidence.

Hence the frequent charge of obscurantism to the Bible believer.

What are we to say to this charge? They have a point. Yes, we *do* believe what God says without the empirical proof that the Bible is true. We believe in the full inspiration of the Bible, that it was written under the infallible guidance of the Holy Spirit (2 Tim. 3:16; 2 Pet. 1:21). We believe we will go to heaven when we die because Jesus Christ paid our debt on the cross by His blood. We admit that these things we believe cannot be proved at the empirical level.

Then why believe it? I reply: the power of the gospel by the illumination of the Holy Spirit persuades one in his or her heart so definitely and convincingly that they would stake their life on it a thousand times! John Calvin called it the inner testimony of the Holy Spirit. As St. Augustine put it a long time ago, it is *faith seeking understanding*. We start with faith; understanding follows. And the understanding really does follow! The understanding comes in ever-increasing measure. "The path of the righteous is like the first gleam of dawn, shining ever brighter till the full light of day" (Prov. 4:18). "Whether you turn to the right or to the left, your ears will hear a voice behind you, saying, 'This is the way; walk in it'" (Isa. 30:21). "Trust in the LORD with all your heart and lean not on your own understanding" (Prov. 3:5).

This makes no sense to the critical cynic. But this is God's chosen way by which *He Himself* will be believed. He chose it that way.

KNOWN ONLY BY FAITH

God could have chosen many different ways to reveal Himself in an undoubted way to men and women. The apostle Paul noted that God might have considered *wisdom* as the way—appealing to the intellectuals of this world. But decreeing wisdom (rather than faith) as the way people were to be saved was rejected by Him.

> For since in the wisdom of God the world through its
> wisdom did not know him, God was pleased through
> the foolishness of what was preached to save those
> who believe.
>
> —1 CORINTHIANS 1:21

In other words, God's wisdom was not to let wisdom become the vehicle by which we are brought to know Him.

God could have used signs and wonders to do it, and sometimes He does use signs and wonders to create faith. (See Acts 13:12.) But, like it or not, according to Paul, God ordained that *faith*—believing the message of the gospel— would be the only way by which people would be saved. This comes through preaching, teaching, witnessing—spreading the good news of Jesus dying on a cross to save us by our testimony—as the way people would know God. It is the folly of what is preached—a message that makes no sense to the erudite, educated, and sophisticated.

> God chose the foolish things of the world to shame
> the wise; God chose the weak things of the world to
> shame the strong. He chose the lowly things of this
> world and the despised things—and the things that
> are not—to nullify the things that are, so that no one
> may boast before him.
>
> —1 CORINTHIANS 1:27–29

This is God's point of view. It makes no sense to us. But more than that, God sovereignly chooses, effectually calls, and converts less impressive people of this world. He deliberately seeks out those who give sophisticated people a reason to look down their noses on the Christian faith. You would have thought that, surely, God would seek out the rich, the famous, the intellects, the wealthy, the philosophers, the scientists, the educated, the cultured, the aristocratic, and royalty. But no. Quite the opposite:

> Think of what you were when you were called. Not many of you were wise by human standards; not many were influential; not many were of noble birth. But God chose the foolish things of the world...
>
> —1 Corinthians 1:26–27

That is the way it was from the moment God chose a virgin in Nazareth to carry the Son of God in her womb. He chose an unknown girl from a town with no good reputation. After Jesus was born, God chose shepherds to be the first to see the Christ child. After Jesus began His ministry, He chose the most unlikely people to be His disciples. The common people heard Him gladly. He attracted sinners rather than the righteous to hang out with Him. This infuriated those in strategic power—the Sadducees and the Pharisees. Moreover, soon after Jesus was raised from the dead, He revealed Himself first of all to Mary Magdalene, a convert who did not have a great reputation (Mark 16:9)—a witness that few if any would believe!

WHEN FAITH IS NO
LONGER POSSIBLE

But when Jesus comes a second time, the possibility of faith will be totally and forever removed. No faith will be needed then. Or possible. For when Jesus comes the second time—"with the clouds, every eye will see him, even those who pierced him; and all the peoples of the earth will mourn because of him" (Rev. 1:7)—faith will not be possible. The high and the mighty, the sophisticated and the lowly, kings and paupers will openly *wail* when they see Jesus in His power and glory. They will see, yes; *every eye will see Him.* You might say they will certainly believe then! But their belief cannot be called *faith.* Seeing is not believing; it will be too late to have true faith then.

It is a great privilege to be able to believe. The kindest thing that can happen on this planet is for God to give you time to believe Him—that is, relying on Him without the tangible evidence you got it right. The worst thing that God can do to a person is to remove the possibility of true faith from him or her.

This therefore means that God would remove the possibility of faith by answering your question now—why does He allow evil and suffering? I therefore implore you to accept this—be thankful that He has not answered your question. Were He to answer this question, you could no longer have true faith. He withholds the answer to be gracious to you and give you faith.

GOD'S PERSPECTIVE MIRRORED IN JESUS

This is why Jesus said to His disciples, "Lazarus is dead, and for your sake I am glad I was not there [to heal Lazarus in Bethany where he was dying], *so that you may believe*" (John 11:14–15, emphasis added). Jesus was taking instructions from the Father. Jesus said earlier, "I tell you the truth, the Son can do nothing by himself; he can do only what he sees his Father doing, because whatever the Father does the Son also does" (John 5:19). The Father in heaven orchestrated all that Jesus ever did on this earth. Therefore it was not merely Jesus teaching His disciples to have faith; God the Father was at the bottom of it all.

Jesus and Lazarus had been close friends. So too were Mary and Martha, Lazarus's sisters. All four of them were close—like family. Therefore when Lazarus was struck with an illness, Mary sent word to Jesus, who was miles away, "Lord, the one you love is sick" (John 11:3). It never crossed Mary's mind that Jesus would refuse to answer her request. Mary assumed that Jesus would stop what He was doing and come to Bethany like a shot to heal her sick brother—and thus keep him from dying.

Jesus Said and Did Things
That Made No Sense

Jesus then began to make comments to His twelve disciples that made no sense. First, He said, "This sickness will not end in death. No, it is for God's glory so that God's Son may be glorified through it" (John 11:4). The truth is, Lazarus died. Second, John, the author of the fourth Gospel, commented that Jesus loved Martha, Mary, and Lazarus. "*Yet when He heard that Lazarus was sick, He stayed where he was* two more days" (v. 6, emphasis added). This did not add up. If Jesus truly loved them, why did He not heed Mary's request, leave where He was immediately, and go to Bethany to heal Lazarus? Third, Jesus said, "Our friend Lazarus has fallen asleep; but I am going there to wake him up" (v. 11). His disciples assumed Jesus mean physical sleep and said, "Lord, if he sleeps, he will get better." Jesus Himself did not tell what He meant by sleep, but John noted that Jesus was actually speaking of Lazarus's death (v. 12). Fourth, Jesus then said plainly, "Lazarus is dead" (v. 14). Whatever was going on?

The Twelve were no doubt perplexed that Jesus did not heal Lazarus. He could have done it by going to Bethany immediately or even healed Lazarus by remote control. (Jesus did not need to be physically present to perform a miracle, as He did in Matthew 8:5–13.) His disciples were confused that Jesus let Lazarus die. It made no sense, whereupon He said to them, "For your sake I am glad I was not there [in Bethany], so *that you may believe*. But let us go to him" (John 11:14, emphasis added). There are more details of this story in John 11 in my book *The Unfailing Love of Jesus*.

Jesus showed up in Bethany four days after the funeral. Martha and Mary did not greet Jesus with a warm welcome but frankly stated, "Lord, if you had been here, my brother would not have died." (See John 11:21, 32.) It was an accusation. They felt majorly let down. Perhaps betrayed. They knew that Lazarus's death was preventable; Jesus could so easily have healed their brother. They told Him so.

JESUS DID NOT REBUKE MARY AND MARTHA FOR THEIR COMMENTS

What interests me is that Jesus did not scold them for expressing their feelings. He wept with them instead. You and I may learn from this that God is not upset with us when we have questions, especially when we ask why. Martha and Mary mirrored man's subjective point of view; Jesus showed God's perspective. He was not threatened, rebuffed, indignant, or disappointed with them. He knew *exactly* what they were feeling.

What amazes me even more is that Jesus openly wept

with them even though He knew that moments later He would perform one of the greatest miracles ever done! He might have said to Mary and Martha, "Shhhh...stop that crying, I am getting ready to raise your brother from the dead." But no. *He wept with them.* God is like that with us. He knows what is future, what is coming ahead, but He realizes *we* don't know and lives with us in our present moment of bewilderment and sorrow. Isn't that wonderful—that our God is like that?

We learn from this story too that there is a divine strategy in unanswered prayer. Have you ever thanked God for *unanswered* prayer? If you haven't, you probably will one day. The account of Jesus not healing Lazarus is proof that unanswered prayer may well mean that God has something better in mind for us than we ourselves had. Mary and Martha could not have seen this during the time of their distress. Jesus eventually vindicated His strategy that initially made no sense by demonstrating that raising Lazarus from the dead was a better idea than keeping him from dying. Would you not agree?

And Jesus's strategy was as much for the Twelve as it was for Mary and Martha. God wanted to teach the disciples what it means to *believe.* In the Gospel of John we have the account of Jesus turning the water into wine (John 2:1–11), the healing of the man at the pool of Bethesda (John 5:1–15), the feeding of the five thousand (John 6:5–13), and the healing of the man who was blind from birth (John 9:1–7). None of these miracles required faith on the part of the Twelve. Jesus did it all by Himself. But when it came to the illness of Lazarus, our Lord wanted the disciples to participate in what was to follow. As Jesus knew exactly what He was going to do when there wasn't enough bread to feed the five thousand (John 6:6), so He planned from the beginning that He would raise Lazarus from the dead. That is why He said that this sickness will not end in death (John 11:4), although it *appeared* to end in death when Lazarus in fact died.

Nearly everybody has heard of Yogi Berra in some way or another. Americans know him as the legendary baseball catcher of the New York Yankees. Most Brits know about the cartoon character Yogi Bear—named after the famed baseball player. And yet Yogi Berra in some ways became even better known by his famous quips. One of them was: "It ain't over 'til it's over."[1] By that he meant that a game is not finished until the very last second when a team has finally won or lost. Don't tell the score in the middle of the ball game—or before it is completely over, one might say. So with Lazarus's illness and God's strategy in letting him die. It wasn't over until it was over, namely, when Jesus unexpectedly, surprisingly, sovereignly, miraculously, and gloriously raised Lazarus from the dead (John 11:44). That is why he could say that Lazarus's sickness would not end in death.

It's not over until it's over. Jesus had the last word. God will have the last word when "every knee should bow, in heaven and on earth and under the earth, and every tongue confess that Jesus Christ is Lord, to the glory of God the Father" (Phil. 2:10–11). Nobody knew what Jesus was up to when He refused to heal Lazarus. Neither can you and I know what God is up to when He allows things to happen that make no sense. But our Lord did all this in order that the Twelve might believe—that is, trust in God's integrity to do the right thing and not panic in the meantime. "I am glad I was not there, so that you may believe" (John 11:15).

Dear reader, there is rhyme and reason to God's universe. There is purpose in all that is going on. Things do not make sense to us now. But behind all that has happened is a sovereign strategy by a loving, caring, omnipotent Father. He will clear His name one day. Let's clear His name now—by faith.

> O Joy, that seekest me through pain,
> I cannot close my heart to Thee;
> I trace the rainbow through the rain,
> And feel the promise is not vain,
> That morn shall tearless me.[2]
>
> —George Matheson (1842–1906)

CHAPTER FIVE

The Way He Is

If you are pleased with me, teach me your ways.

—Exodus 33:13

God moves in a mysterious way His wonders to perform;
He plants His footsteps in the sea, and rides upon the storm.

—William Cowper (1731–1800)

I T IS OFTEN said we get our notions about God from our parents, especially our dads. I am sure there is a lot of truth in this. For example, those who have harsh fathers see God as harsh; those whose fathers are distant and never around have difficulty believing that God listens to them. I can remember walking home from school when I was eight years old with a report card with eight As and two Bs, and I knew my dad would say more about the two Bs, that he would say, "Study harder, RT, and next time you will have all As"—and I was right. The consequence has been that I never felt I could do quite enough to please my dad, and

I have had this hang-up also about God, that I might not come up to His lofty standard. If I am totally candid, I still struggle in this area.

My upbringing in my old church in Kentucky was in the context of a lot of noise (people shouted for joy—the preachers yelled to be heard), strict legalistic lifestyle, being afraid that any day I could go to hell and believing that my getting to heaven had everything to do with how good I was. And yet, believe it or not, I am not entirely unhappy about my church background, for not all was bad. The very thing that initially intrigued Dr. Martyn Lloyd-Jones about me was my Nazarene background. Despite the rather negative things I just mentioned, I developed a healthy fear of God, a strong belief in the Bible, a love for prayer, and an immense desire to get close to God.

The most profound thing one can say about God is that *He is as He is because that is the way He is.* He did not make Himself a certain way; He always was and is like He is. When Moses asked to know the name of God, the reply came: "I AM WHO I AM. This is what you are to say to the Israelites: 'I AM has sent me to you'" (Exod. 3:14). The Hebrew name for God is *Yahweh*—I am that I am. Dr. N. Burnett Magruder, one of my chief mentors—and the man who preached my ordination sermon in 1964—used to say that the deepest thing you can say about God is that *He is.*

The Bible is all about this God. So when I refer to *God*, I mean the God of the Bible, the One revealed in it and talked about in it. He is the uncreated Creator who always was, is, and shall ever be. He made what is visible because He *chose* to do so and did it by His Word (Gen. 1:1–3; Heb. 11:3). He is before all things, which means that before He created anything, there was nothing there but God. He created the world in a manner so that it was "subjected to frustration" (Rom. 8:20), "futility" (ESV), "vanity" (KJV), "made unable to attain its purpose" (JB). This allowed for the possibility of evil in the world. Since God created all things, it included the devil (Col. 1:16). At an appointed time God decreed, He sent His Son into the world—which was roughly 2,100 years ago; the eternal Word who was God became flesh and therefore was given a body (John 1:1, 14; Gal. 4:4; Heb. 10:5). He was given the name Jesus (Matt. 1:21). When Jesus died on the cross, it was not because things went wrong but because things went right, this being why He came into the world in the first place (Acts 2:23; 4:28). This same Jesus was raised from the dead and ascended to the right hand of God the Father, where He is right now as you read these lines (Acts 2:33). He will remain there until the day the Father orders His return to the earth to reign and be the supreme judge (Acts 17:31; 2 Tim. 4:1).

THE ATTRIBUTES OF GOD

The word *attribute* means an inherent characteristic or feature of someone. God has certain unchangeable characteristics, all of which make up His being; they are, indeed, unchangeable. In fact, one of God's attributes is that *He cannot change*: "I the LORD do not change" (Mal. 3:6; James 1:17). He is *eternal*, having no beginning or end (Ps. 90:2; Rev. 1:8.) He is *infinite* (unlimited—Ps. 145:3; Isa. 40:28). God is also *triune*: one God in three persons—Father, Son, and Holy Spirit (Matt. 28:19; 2 Cor. 13:14). Another characteristic of God is that *He cannot lie* (Heb. 6:18; Titus 1:2). That is the way He *is*.

There are other attributes: He is *omnipotent* (all-powerful—Jer. 32:17; Luke 1:37), *omniscient* (He knows everything—Job 37:16; Heb. 4:13), *omnipresent* (He is everywhere—Ps. 139:1–12; Jer. 23:24), *invisible* (Exod. 33:20; John 1:18), *light* (1 Tim. 6:16; 1 John 1:5), *inscrutable* (impossible to grasp or figure out—Job 11:7; Rom. 11:33); *pure* and *holy* (Lev. 11:44; Hab. 1:13), *all-wise* (Ps. 147:5; Rom. 11:33–34), *sovereign* (having the right to choose according to the purpose of His will—Rom. 9:11–15; Eph. 1:11), *just* (Deut. 32:4; Eccles. 12:14), *love* (John 3:16; 1 John 4:8), *merciful* (Ps. 145:8; Luke 6:36); *jealous* (Exod. 34:14; Deut. 5:9), and capable of demonstrating *wrath* (Ps. 2:12; Matt. 3:7).

Sum Total of His Attributes

There is one word, however, that summarizes the above, this being the sum total of all His attributes: *glory*. God is essentially a God of glory (Acts 7:2). If you had to pick one word that mirrors God's nature or His essence, it is *glory*. The Hebrew word translated "glory" is *kabhod*—meaning heaviness or weightiness, showing His immense stature. The Greek word is *doxa*—praise or glory, coming from a root word that means opinion. God's glory is His opinion or will. When you combine the Hebrew *kabhod* with the Greek *doxa* you get several words that point to the majesty, loftiness, splendor, power, wisdom, purpose, and sovereign will of God. And yet all these brought down to one word is *glory*.

This is why God is a jealous God; His name is Jealous (Exod. 34:14). The first of the Ten Commandments is: "You shall have no other gods before me" (Exod. 20:3). He will not tolerate any rival or anyone who elbows in on His territory; He wants the total credit for our salvation and also for the good we do. He wants our total allegiance to Him. This is why He wants to be worshiped, praised, and honored. This is the way He is.

God's Idiosyncrasies

What I have stated above regarding God's attributes is nothing new; it is standard orthodox Christian teaching about God. But I now want to describe other characteristics of God—perhaps less known. What follows are His special, unusual—perhaps peculiar and certainly idiosyncratic—ways. We may or may not like His ways. But He is the only true God there is; He is like He is because that is the way He is. I say it again: He could not be anything different even if He wanted to change. But not to worry; He is happy with Himself.

Moses said to God, "If you are pleased with me, *teach me your ways*" (Exod. 33:13, emphasis added). I was greatly sobered when I once read this. I remember seeing it as if for the first time. When Moses discerned that God was pleased with him, he decided to exploit this—and put in a request. In that moment Moses could probably have asked for and received *anything* he wanted. Have you ever fanaticized what *you* might ask for God to do if you knew you could have *anything* you wanted? That is why Moses's request sobered me as it did. It made me wish I had thought to ask God, "Teach me your ways," but I didn't. This lets you know what kind of man Moses was and why God was so pleased with him.

Solomon had a similar experience, having been invited by God to ask for anything. It was his chance to ask for the moon, sun, and stars! He asked for *wisdom*. God was so pleased with that request that He promised Solomon he would get not only the wisdom he asked for but also things he didn't ask for—long life, wealth, and other blessings (1 Kings 3:10–13). It goes to show that if we pray in God's will—for example, seeking first His kingdom and righteousness—He will give us more than we even wished for (Matt. 6:33; Eph. 3:20).

So when Moses might have asked for the earth and sky, he asked instead to know *God's ways*. This pleased God more than ever that Moses wanted this. It honored God no end that Moses loved Him *so* much that he wanted to be taught God's *ways*.

One of the things that gave God great pain and heartache was that His ancient people "have not known *my ways*" (Ps. 95:10; Heb. 3:10, emphasis added). God wants us to know His *ways*—to see how much we will love Him when we learn more about Him, including His idiosyncrasies. God wants us to affirm Him *as He is*, not what we may wish He were like.

Totally forgiving God, then, consists in letting Him off the hook not only for what He does but also for being the kind of God He is. This means accepting God with His aforementioned attributes but also His idiosyncrasies, some of which we now observe.

HE HIDES HIMSELF
WITHOUT WARNING

"Truly you are a God who hides himself, O God and Savior of Israel" (Isa. 45:15). It is only a matter of time that we all find out what Isaiah discovered—that the same God who had been so real, vibrant, and seemingly close to us yesterday suddenly disappears today. He quietly and, without notice, moves away from us as if He had never been present in the first place. Here today, gone tomorrow. Why? You tell me. But if pushed to answer I would say it is partly to keep us from becoming overly familiar with Him. God does desire intimacy with us but not to the degree we can take Him for granted. It is part of His nature, as I said before, to play hard-to-get. He wants to be pursued. This is the way He is.

We can learn from the children of Israel as they were entering into the Promised Land. They were required to keep themselves from getting too close to the ark of the covenant. They were, however, instructed to *follow the ark* and the priests who were carrying it in order to know which way to go. But they were at the same time told to "*keep a distance of about a thousand yards* between you and the ark; do not go near it" (Josh. 3:2–4, emphasis added).

One of God's ways is that He wants us to draw nigh to Him, but sometimes we can become a little too familiar with Him. We can also take Him for granted, not unlike

Joseph and Mary thinking Jesus was with them when in fact they carried on for a day and He was not with them at all (Luke 2:44).

God does not want to be taken for granted, and I reckon one of the reasons He hides Himself is to keep us from being presumptuous.

If only God would give us advance notice that He will shortly be hiding His face from us. I wish He might say, "Next Tuesday afternoon about three o'clock, you will notice I will suddenly withdraw the light of My countenance from you. But do not worry; do not panic. I will only be testing you." But no. *He just does it.* He even sometimes does this to His newest convert, cutting short the honeymoon. He does this with His most mature children. He does this especially with those earmarked for a gigantic task. When Samuel poured the anointing oil on young David (1 Sam. 16:13), He might have said, "David, I need to tell you that it will be another twenty years before you will be crowned king. One more thing: you will be spending the next twenty years running from your enemy Saul just to stay alive. But not to worry; it is part of your preparation." But no. David, without any warning, was thrust into an unimaginable era of mistreatment and injustice within a very short period of time. It lasted for twenty years.

God does desire intimacy with us. "The LORD confides

in those who fear him" (Ps. 25:14). Part of this confidence has to do with our willingness *never to tell* everything He shares with us. Joseph had prophetic dreams that indicated his brothers would bow down to him one day. His mistake was telling them these dreams (Gen. 37:5–9)! When God said, "If I were hungry I would not tell you" (Ps. 50:12), it was dead giveaway that He *wanted* to share His heart with someone.

What then does God want us to do when He hides Himself? Answer: to seek His face. As I said, He wants to be pursued. "You have said, 'Seek my face.' My heart says to you, 'Your face, LORD, do I seek. Hide not your face from me" (Ps. 27:8–9, ESV). The Lord understands every heart and understands every motive behind the thoughts. "If you seek him, he will be found by you" (1 Chron. 28:9). "You will seek me and find me, when you seek me with all your heart. I will be found by you" (Jer. 29:13–14).

Sometimes it is our sins that are at the bottom of God hiding His face. "Your iniquities have separated you from your God; your sins have hidden his face from you, so that he will not hear" (Isa. 59:2). But God does this because He is jealous; He loves us and wants us to pursue Him. Hiding His face is one way to get our attention so we will seek His face. "If my people, who are called by my name, will humble themselves and pray and seek my face and turn from their wicked ways, then will I hear from heaven and will forgive their sin and will heal their land" (2 Chron. 7:14).

What is it like when God hides Himself? We feel unloved. Alone. We feel we must have been deceived, even imagining He had been real to us before. We pray and pray and pray without any answer or a hint of response. He may put His people through a time of drought—without rain. He may withhold timely words to us exactly when we need so much to hear from Him. The worst kind of famine is a famine of hearing the words of the Lord (Amos 8:11). He may let His own people sink to such depths that the surrounding community and nations have no respect for them—e.g., the church—whatever. He may allow His church—the apple of His eye—to become the laughingstock of the world. He may withhold leadership ability from the leaders and keep those in authority and influence devoid of wisdom. He may withhold vindication, financial blessing, health, and protection from those who are called by His name.

But these are not necessarily bad signs; it is His loving jealousy at the bottom of His hiding His face. He longs to get us to seek His face, that He may truly get our attention.

He Loves to Show Up
in the Nick of Time

I don't understand it, but God has a habit of hiding His face so we are left wondering if we will ever see it again. This hiding often takes place beyond our apparent point of endurance. And then He shows up. He called Moses to rescue the children of Israel and then brought on more suffering than ever. Those Israelites who had been building the ancient pyramids for Pharaoh had been mistreated for a long time. But right after Moses came to help them, things went from bad to worse! Pharaoh made it harder than ever for them! "Now get to work. You will not be given any straw [to make bricks], yet you must produce your full quota of bricks," said Pharaoh (Exod. 5:18).

Talk about feeling let down! Or (possibly) betrayed. Moses then cried to God, "O Lord, why have you brought trouble upon this people? Is this why you sent me? Ever since I went to Pharaoh to speak in your name, he has brought trouble upon this people, and *you have not rescued your people at all"* (Exod. 5:22–23, emphasis added). Moses was utterly bewildered. But he did not give up. He persisted.

There eventually followed the ten plagues upon Egypt that finally resulted in Pharaoh letting the people of Israel leave the area. But three days later the Egyptians began to pursue Moses and his people. The Israelites had been led to a corner near the Red Sea. They dared not go back to where they were, and they could not go to the right or left. Only the sea was before them. "As Pharaoh approached, the Israelites looked up, and there were the Egyptians, marching after them. They were terrified and cried out to the LORD" (Exod. 14:10).

The Israelites then turned on Moses: "Was it because there were no graves in Egypt that you brought us to the desert to die? What have you done to us by bringing us out of Egypt?" (v. 11). Moses seemed so brave: "Do not be afraid. Stand firm and you will see the deliverance the LORD will bring you today.... The LORD will fight for you; you need only to be still" (vv. 13–14). But behind this seemingly courageous exterior Moses himself was apparently scared to death! A verse that might have read—but isn't there, could have read: "*Moses cried out to the Lord.*" All I know is that the Lord said to Moses, "Why are you crying out to me? Tell the Israelites to move one. Raise your staff and stretch out your hand over the sea to divide the water so that the Israelites can go through the sea on dry ground" (vv. 15–16).

They did. It all happened at the last minute. I do not know why but sometimes God does things at five minutes to twelve—just when we think it is too late. It's not over until it's over. God is like that; it is the way He is, this being one of His idiosyncrasies.

In 1962–1963, as I mentioned earlier, I was pastor of a

church in Ohio—the church where I saw my dad in a vision. Most of these people rejected my teaching; many stopped giving so we would be forced to leave (it worked). I will never forget one morning when we got up, I wondered how Louise and I would make it through the day. Our meager salary (one hundred dollars a week) had been cut virtually in half. We had to pay our house rent out of an even smaller salary. We had no fuel for our car, no groceries. But when the mail came that day, there was a check for twenty-five dollars. It was sent by a couple in Illinois. I didn't even know they knew we were in Ohio. They both woke up the day before with a conviction they should send Louise and me twenty-five dollars. It was pure gold to us. It is another example that God is *never too late, never too early, but always just on time.*

His Unpredictable Manifestations

When God does show up, it is often by manifesting Himself in undoubted but surprising—sometimes odd—ways. He led Israel through the wilderness by a cloud "over the tabernacle by day, and fire was in the cloud by night" (Exod. 40:38). When the cloud lifted, they moved. If it didn't, they stayed where they were. The people Israel lived that way for forty years.

One day God showed up with the prophet Elijah being at rock bottom of discouragement. He told Elijah that the Lord was about to pass by. "Then a great and powerful wind tore the mountains apart and shattered the rocks before the LORD, but the LORD was not in the wind. After the wind there was an earthquake, but the LORD was not in the earthquake. After the earthquake came a fire, but the LORD was not in the fire. And after the fire came a gentle whisper" (1 Kings 19:11–12; KJV—"still small voice").

That was the way God chose to show up on that occasion. "When Elijah heard it, he pulled his cloak over his face and went out and stood at the mouth of the cave" (v. 13).

There were times when smoke appeared in the ancient temple, when the temple was filled with a cloud and "priests could not perform their service because of the cloud, for the glory of the LORD filled the temple" (2 Chron. 5:14). An extraordinary service at my old church in Ashland, Kentucky, in April 1956 was accompanied by a haze that filled the auditorium—very possibly the same phenomenon. This is certainly an unusual manifestation.

Sometimes God shows up with a healing presence, as when "the power of the Lord was present for him to heal the sick" (Luke 5:17). Sometimes the presence of God brings great fear, as when the lives of Ananias and Sapphira were suddenly taken right after they lied to the Holy Spirit (Acts

5:1–11). Sometimes the presence of the Lord calls for joy (Neh. 8:10). There was great joy in Samaria when people were healed (Acts 8:8). Sometimes the presence of the Lord causes people to fall to the ground (John 18:6; Rev. 1:17).

Isaiah exhorted us to "seek the LORD while He may be *found*" (Isa. 55:6, emphasis added). Said David, "Let everyone who is godly pray to you while you may be *found*" (Ps. 32:6, emphasis added). When He hides Himself, one feels his or her prayers are not getting anywhere. But when He shows up, it is a moment to seize. "Sow for yourselves righteousness, reap the fruit of unfailing love, and break up your unplowed ground; for it is time to seek the LORD, until he comes and showers righteousness on you" (Hosea 10:12). Such an exhortation by the prophet was a timely sign that God was nearby—preparing to show up.

We used to pray in Westminster Chapel for a manifestation of God's glory in our midst along with an ever-increasing openness in us to the way He chose to show up. Knowing a little bit about church history, I sometimes feared that God would come to our traditional church in London in a manner that would be hard to accept! In 1801 in my state of Kentucky at the beginning of the camp meeting phenomenon in an area called Cane Ridge, a Methodist lay preacher stood on a fallen tree before fifteen thousand people. He took his text from 2 Corinthians 5:10, that we must all stand before the judgment seat of Christ to give an account of the things done in the body whether good or bad. The fear of the Lord in great power fell on the people. Unexpectedly hundreds fell helplessly to the ground, lying that way for hours. They all eventually came up shouting with new assurance and joy while others fell to the ground. This lasted nonstop for four days. Since I feared this might happen at Westminster Chapel, I worded our prayer covenant petition as I did!

GOD LOVES TO FAVOR THE UNDERDOG

A long time ago God set a pattern of choosing people for service nobody would have dreamed of. He loves to select the person we may think to be the least likely to be used by Him. In the case of young David, his own father, Jesse, totally underestimated him. It never entered Jesse's mind that David would be chosen. When Samuel came to the house of Jesse to anoint a new king (while King Saul was still alive), Jesse happily called out seven of his sons from whom the prophet Samuel would choose, beginning with Eliab the firstborn. None of these sons, however, were chosen after Samuel looked at each one of them. "Are these all the sons you have?" Samuel asked Jesse. "'There is still the youngest,' Jesse answered, 'but he is tending the sheep'" (1 Sam. 16:11).

Jesse seemed uncomfortable with Samuel's probing, as Jesse apparently had not planned to bring David into the picture at all. No one could have guessed that the next king would be David, son of Jesse.

Jesus continued this pattern from the beginning of His ministry—reaching out to those who heretofore had been overlooked, especially the underdog. He sent a signal to John the Baptist how to know the true Messiah: "The blind receive sight, the lame walk, those who have leprosy are cured, the deaf hear, the dead are raised, and the good news is *preached to the poor*" (Luke 7:22, emphasis added). Not only did the common people hear Jesus gladly, but, as we saw earlier, Jesus intentionally chose for His disciples men who seemed to be the least likely to qualify for this. Instead of picking men from among the Sadducees and Pharisees—those who had the greatest prestige—He chose ordinary men, some of whom raised eyebrows such as Matthew, a tax collector.

Not only that, a typical accusation leveled at Jesus was that He kept company with sinners. Jesus pleaded guilty to the charge and then gave three parables that demonstrated how God loves to save people who offend righteous people (Luke 15). When His disciples were asked by the Pharisees, "Why does your teacher eat with tax collectors and 'sinners'?," Jesus replied: "It is not the healthy who need a doctor, but the sick.... For I have not come to call the righteous, but sinners" (Matt. 9:11–13).

Sinners. The poor. The unknown. The rejected. Those who are hurt. Those who most people don't want to have anything to do with. They are the very ones whom God seeks out and favors. And whatever differences Paul may have had with certain Jewish leaders, they agreed on this: "That we should continue to remember the poor, the very thing I was eager to do," said Paul (Gal. 2:10). They are the very kind of people God loves to turn His attention to. "Religion that God our Father accepts as pure and faultless is this: to look after orphans and widows in their distress and to keep oneself from being polluted by the world" (James 1:27).

Jesus seeks those who are rejected, hurting, bruised, and broken. Are you bruised? Are you broken? Have you been rejected? Jesus calls for you. "A bruised reed he will not break, a smoldering wick he will not snuff out" (Matt. 12:20).

It is another one of God's ways; one of His idiosyncrasies.

This is the true God. "The LORD is righteous in all his ways and loving toward all he has made" (Ps. 145:17). The Lord says: "Let him who boasts boast about this: that he understands and *knows me*, that I am the LORD, who exercises kindness, justice and righteousness on earth, for in these I delight" (Jer. 9:24, emphasis added).

That is the way He is.

CHAPTER SIX

God's Reply to Habakkuk

For the revelation awaits an appointed time; it speaks of the end and will not prove false. Though it linger, wait for it; it will certainly come and not delay...but the righteous will live by his faith.

—HABAKKUK 2:3–4

Faith is a living, daring confidence in God's grace, so sure and certain that a man could stake his life on it a thousand times.

—MARTIN LUTHER (1483–1546)

EARLIER IN THIS book we looked at the prophet Habakkuk's complaints. You may recall that he complained that (1) God doesn't listen, (2) He doesn't see what is going on, (3) He doesn't care, and (4) He knowingly permits evil to thrive and doesn't even seem to mind that His own law is being treated with contempt. God was apparently doing nothing about it.

A Surprising Reply

God did answer Habakkuk, but the answer didn't please Habakkuk. The prophet was not prepared for what God was going to do, namely, "something in your days that you would not believe, even if you were told" (Hab. 1:5). A quick glance at a word like that smacks of something great, exciting, and wonderful that is about to happen. "Oh, good," Habakkuk must have thought. That is, until God revealed what that *something* was: "I am raising up the Babylonians, that ruthless and impetuous people" (v. 6). This meant that the Babylonians, Judah's enemy, were moving in soon to take over—and with God being totally behind it! In other words, the reply from God would seem worse than the problem! Habakkuk might wish he had not asked. But this was the revelation: God was going to use the Babylonians to cure Judah of their idolatry!

That is why Habakkuk recorded his prophecy and why it is a book in the canon of Scripture. It turns out that God had indeed carefully observed *all* that Habakkuk was crying out about. God only appeared not to listen; He only seemed to have His back turned. However, Habakkuk was not pleased with God's answer, namely, that God was going to send the Babylonians and bring Judah into captivity. Habakkuk was no doubt hoping God would step in and bring an *end* to the evil that was rampant in his day. But his specific request was at least for an *explanation* of what was going on. "Why do you make me look at injustice? Why do you tolerate wrong?" (v. 3).

Here is what is interesting: God's solution or explanation was nowhere near to what Habakkuk expected or wanted. It is so often like that. In our limited knowledge, we come to conclusions as to the only way forward or for a reasonable explanation of things. God's ways are higher than our ways, His thoughts higher than our thoughts (Isa. 55:8–9). It turns out that God was not only aware of all that was going on in Judah, but He also had a strategy fully in place. The revelation of that strategy—which God gave to Habakkuk—actually meant that things in Jerusalem and Judah would go from very, very bad to much, much worse. What is known as the Babylonian captivity was next on God's agenda for Judah.

This word to Habakkuk apparently came around 600 B.C. Approximately fourteen years later—in 586 B.C.—the Babylonians invaded Jerusalem and marched the people of Judah to Babylon. The nightmarish vision was literally fulfilled. God's strategy was this: He would use the Babylonians to get Judah's attention—to drive them back to God. Why? Apparently nothing else would work. But no one dreamed of such a way forward.

HABAKKUK'S
SECOND COMPLAINT

Having been displeased by God's reply to Habakkuk's first complaint, his complaint was followed by another: "Your eyes are too pure to look on evil; you cannot tolerate wrong. Why then do you tolerate the treacherous? Why are you silent while the wicked swallow up those more righteous than themselves?" (Hab. 1:13). Habakkuk could not conceive of the Most Holy God using wicked men to punish Judah. Granted that Judah has been in disobedience, but surely the Babylonians were much, much worse! "O Rock, you have ordained them [the Babylonians] to punish" (v. 12). It is possible that God's answer went against Habakkuk's theology, for Habakkuk could not see how a most holy God could use evil people to punish His beloved people. Habakkuk was not only a prophet but also an eloquent poet; in verses 14 to 17 he poetically pleads with God not to continue with this strategy. Habakkuk movingly urges God to see it his way. The poetry summed up means: *This cannot be right! You surely cannot do such a thing!*

HABAKKUK'S
PERSISTENT FAITH

So God answered the prophet Habakkuk's first complaint. It simply did not satisfy Habakkuk. It made no sense to him. I do not know if Habakkuk felt betrayed that God would suddenly raise up the Babylonians to attack His covenant people. I only know that Habakkuk persisted in seeking God's face. He did not give up. He pressed on.

That is what you and I must do when God makes no sense to us.

Perhaps you and I would feel the same way Habakkuk felt if we got God's answer to what may be happening in our lives at the moment, which we do not understand. Let down. Confused. Perhaps disillusioned for a while. But we know that if we seek the Lord with all our hearts, He will answer us; He has promised to do so. But we may or may not like His answer. Habakkuk did not like the answer he got, but he didn't give up on God!

How would you feel if God responded to your plea by letting things go from very bad to much worse? How would I feel? How do I know how I would cope if I were in an extreme suffering beyond which I have ever experienced? My own suffering is a minute indeed compared to situations I know about and probably would not compare with the suffering of some who read these lines. So how would I respond? I don't know for sure. I would only *hope* I would practice what I preach. In any case, this writer is not up on a pedestal looking down his nose at you. I don't know what I would do if I were in your shoes. I can only sympathize with you—most sincerely—and yet ask you to consider that God has a strategy that will satisfy you at the end of the day.

GOD'S ANSWER TO HABAKKUK'S SECOND COMPLAINT

The prophet Habakkuk is an example of persistent faith. He promised to stand and watch, waiting to see what God would say in response to this second complaint: "I will look to see what he will say to me, and what answer I am to give to this complaint" (Hab. 2:1). God responded to Habakkuk's second complaint:

> For the revelation awaits an appointed time; it speaks of the end and will not prove false. Though it linger, wait for it; it will certainly come and will not delay. See, he is puffed up; his desires are not upright—but the righteous will live by his faith.
>
> —HABAKKUK 2:3–4

God's reply summed up was: *Wait.* The answer will eventually come; "it speaks of the end and will not prove false. Though it linger, wait for it; it will certainly come and will not delay" (Hab. 2:3).

You may say this reply from God was like kicking the can down the road, an expression one hears as if to describe a politician who hasn't fully explained his policy; it is buying more time, avoiding an answer. You might say: the answer

Habakkuk received came without giving an immediate solution or explanation.

Wrong. God in fact gave Habakkuk—and all of us—something to live for. God's answer was most profound. Whereas God did not immediately answer the question "Why do you allow evil and suffering?", He guaranteed that the answer *would be coming down the road*. Some might say, "That's not good enough, I want to know *now*."

The truth is, God's reply to Habakkuk dealt with two issues simultaneously: (1) the situation then—in 600 b.c. and (2) things coming in the future. In the meantime God says to wait a while longer.

A CLOSER LOOK AND
EXPLANATION OF HABAKKUK 2:3

"For the revelation." Revelation refers to what God has just revealed to Habakkuk, what has been unveiled. It is also called vision.

"Awaits an appointed time." This means the date has been set for the fulfillment of this revelation; there is nothing one can do to bring it forward. One can only wait.

"It speaks of the end." The Apologetics Study Bible: "It testifies about the end."[1] The end refers to two things simultaneously: (a) how the situation in Habakkuk's day would wind up and

(b) how God would explain things in the end times, on the last day—when He would clear His name.

"And will not prove false." "It will not lie" (ESV). It will be obvious that the ultimate clarification and explanation of God's mysterious ways will be out in the open and unhidden. God's answer will be utterly and completely trustworthy and satisfying.

"Though it linger." "If it seems slow" (ESV). *The Apologetics Study Bible*: "Though it delays."[2] We are told unmistakably in advance that this unveiling would not come in the next day or two. This is so encouraging. God graciously stoops to our weakness, knowing as He does how we want immediate answers. He lets us know it could even be a long time off before we get our questions answered.

"Wait for it." God Himself is saying to all of us: do not give up! Wait.

"It will certainly come." He did not have to add that. But He did. The God who knows our frame and remembers that we are dust now reaches out to us as if to say yet again: don't give up and please know you will not be disappointed. It is like when the Lord said to John on the Isle of Patmos: "Write this down, for these words are trustworthy and true" (Rev. 21:5).

"And will not delay." This means that once God steps in, it will happen quickly, like the twinkling of the eye—faster

than you can bat an eyelash. God will do this suddenly. There will come a time when the waiting is over.

What if you still don't want to wait any longer?

If you keep saying, "I don't want a revelation or explanation down the road; *I want an answer now*," I reply by suggesting the following: though this might be understandably painful for you to accept, God would do you no favor to unveil the reason He allows evil and suffering generally— or why He has let you go through such an ordeal. This is because if He did it, would rule out the opportunity for you to exercise *faith*, as we have previously seen in chapter 4. The only way you and I can be saved is through faith, and the only way we can please God is by faith. Please be patient.

The revelation, then, waits for an appointed time. This means the date was been set. And as I said, there is nothing anybody can do to bring it forward. It speaks of the end. But the revelation isn't finished yet—there is a lot more (Hab. 2:4–20), although we will look mainly at Habakkuk 2:4.

THE GLORIOUS NEWS

In all that Habakkuk was struggling with was God's secret purpose at work. The prophet could not have known that behind all he was feeling was God waiting to unveil the greatest news of human history—the plan of salvation. We are going to look at Habakkuk 2:4 carefully as well. Part of this verse—"the righteous will live by faith" is quoted three times in the New Testament.

Here is a close look and explanation of Habakkuk 2:4:

"*See, he is puffed up; his desires are not upright.*" *The Apologetics Study Bible*: "Look, his ego is inflated; he is without integrity."[3] This is a reference to Judah's enemy—the Babylonians, though referred to as "he" and "his." It is simply God Himself acknowledging what Habakkuk was trying to point out! Habakkuk feared that God was not aware of how vile the enemy—the Babylonians—were, and it did not seem right that God would use such evil people to punish His beloved Judah. God lets Habakkuk know that He fully realizes what Habakkuk is feeling.

"*But the righteous.*" The righteous, in contrast to the wicked Babylonians, are those who have faith. This verse ties straight to Abraham's day. God saw Abraham's faith and immediately imputed—put to his credit—*righteousness* (Gen. 15:6). Habakkuk 2:4 and Genesis 15:6 go together. This points to our salvation—how you and I are saved: by faith.

"*Will live.*" This means that the righteous shall be empowered, energized. It refers to *life* as opposed to death; it means regeneration, being born again. It is equally a reference both to saving faith and persistent faith.

"*By his faith.*" Most versions today have a footnote: that the Hebrew translated "his faith" may also be translated "his faithfulness." But there is more: the "his" is *God's* faithfulness: the righteous shall live by His faithfulness. The New Testament usage demonstrates that Habakkuk 2:4 means the faith or faithfulness of God. Habakkuk 2:4 is quoted three times in the New Testament: Romans 1:17, Galatians 3:11, and Hebrews 10:38. When God told Abraham that his seed would be as numerous as the stars of the heavens and as the sand on the seashore, Abraham actually believed it! That faith counted for righteousness (Gen. 15:6). Habakkuk is merely building on this foundation. It promises this: the righteous shall *live* by relying on God's integrity. Knowing that God is faithful and that He keeps His word is what keeps us going! Faith in God's faithfulness produces life—saving faith; persistent faith in God's faithfulness produces life to the full (John 10:10). Relying on the faithfulness of God is further borne out by the context of its use in Hebrews 10:38. For those wanting a deeper look at the way Habakkuk is applied in Romans 1:17 and Galatians 3:11, see my little book *He Saves*, which shows how we are saved by our faith in the faith, or faithfulness, of Christ (Gal. 2:16, 20, KJV).

Habakkuk wanted an immediate *explanation* from God as to why evil thrived. Instead of getting the explanation, he got a delay. But that delay was the best thing God could have given to Habakkuk and to Israel—and us! That delay opened the way to salvation. It opened the way to please

God. It opened the way by which God would be more fully known. It pointed to the time when God would—at last—clear His name but by bringing us in on it in advance so we can participate in it.

To put it another way: Peter forecasted that scoffers would come in the last days and ask—referring to Jesus's second coming, "Where is this 'coming' He promised? Ever since our fathers died, everything goes on as it has since the beginning of creation" (2 Pet. 3:3–4). It is like people saying, "I've heard all this before. I heard this when I was a child that Jesus could come at any minute. He still hasn't come." I reply: had He come a hundred years ago, *you* would not be here. Had He come fifty years ago, *you* may not have been converted. So if nothing else comes from this lengthy delay, you must admit it has been a definite advantage to you. Is this not true?

The delay of God's explanation—or ending evil—is what makes it possible for us to be saved. The delay is what potentially saves us. The very delay of God, either ending evil or explaining why it doesn't end it, is what makes salvation possible; that is, if we will trust God's faithfulness.

God's integrity is at the bottom of the delayed revelation. We must make a choice—to believe it or not to believe it. It is coming, says Habakkuk. It may linger. It may mean a *long* delay: thousands of years in fact.

When Jesus showed up some two thousand years ago—healing the sick and raising the dead—His followers became convinced that the visible kingdom of God—coming at long last—would mean overthrowing Rome immediately. What is more, it would appear any hour. The multitudes were hoping to make Jesus king when He fed the five thousand (John 6:15). On Palm Sunday they shouted hosanna because this *was*—surely—to be the day He would announce His kingship.

Jesus knew this would not be the case at all. He then gave a parable because He could see how the people thought that He would momentarily reveal His kingly power and command Rome to leave the land that was Israel's. The parable was that of a man of noble birth going to a distant country to be appointed king and then return. Before the nobleman left, he gave his servants money to invest. "Put this money to work until I come back," were his last words to them. But the king did not return very soon. The long delay exposed whether or not the king's subjects would be faithful by how they handled their money. The king eventually returned home and rewarded his subjects in proportion to their carefulness to increase the king's investment in them. Some were given double their investment. One of them invested nothing but hid his money. He was severely judged. (See Luke 19:11–27.)

In any case, Jesus is saying by this parable, Israel's expectations and Jesus's mission were not on the same page. (If you want to see the meaning of this parable in more detail, please see my book *The Parables of Jesus*.)

Habakkuk was given clear notice that the ultimate explanation for what God does that we don't understand would be a long time off. This was 600 B.C. Six hundred years later the Word was made flesh—the coming of Jesus of Nazareth. People thought the end was to come during Jesus's lifetime. Then after Jesus's resurrection His disciples were still obsessed with the idea of His overthrowing Rome: "Lord, are you at this time going to restore the kingdom to Israel?" (Acts 1:6). The cynic might still say Jesus's reply was also kicking the can down the road. He gave the promise of the Holy Spirit. Another delay before the last day. Then came the claim that Jesus had ascended to the right hand of God, an explanation that could never be proved. Another delay. But Jesus also promised His second coming. The ultimate delay! Some of those to whom Paul wrote thought the day had already taken place (2 Thess. 2:2). Paul pointed out certain things that must take place before Jesus can come. People have been speculating ever since. Some still want to predict dates. Jesus cautioned that we do not know the day or the hour when He will come back; only the Father knows (Matt. 24:36).

We may not like it, but God still says to us: *wait*. What are we to do? Live by the faithfulness of God. He who promised is faithful. He won't finally let us down. He never has; He never will.

PART THREE

Another Dimension

The god of this age has blinded the minds of unbelievers, so that they cannot see the light of the gospel of the glory of Christ, who is the image of God.

—2 CORINTHIANS 4:4

The devil can cite Scripture for his purpose.

—WILLIAM SHAKESPEARE

CHAPTER SEVEN

The Accuser

The accuser of our brothers, who accuses them before our God day and night, has been hurled down. And they overcame him by the blood of the Lamb and by the word of their testimony; they did not love their lives so much as to shrink from death.

—REVELATION 12:10–11

Don't believe the devil, even when he tells the truth.

—WILLIAM PERKINS (1558–1602)

I DO NOT LIKE writing about the devil. I hate it in fact. I have never once preached a sermon on the devil or Satan by choice. I only did so when the text called for this, as when I would preach through a book in the Bible. I was once asked to do a couple sermons on spiritual warfare for the London City Mission a number of years ago, but I accepted the invitation reluctantly. I realize that some people feel called to do spiritual warfare, even as part of their rationale for ministry. I could never do this.

There are two extremes that some people fall into when bringing in the devil. One is they obsess on him. I think some see a demon on every bush, talking about him excessively and blaming the devil for every problem—from cancer to the common cold. I have never felt at peace in this perspective. The other extreme is to neglect Satan altogether—as if he doesn't exist. Believe me, he exists. He is also very comfortable with either of these extremes—whether being preoccupied with him or pretending he does not exist.

SIX REASONS FOR BRINGING SATAN INTO THIS BOOK

Why bring such a dark matter into this book? For six reasons. First, the devil is the great accuser. Whereas his primary objective is to accuse us who are believers—to give us a terrible guilt trip by throwing up our past sins (Rev. 12:10–12), he equally would *accuse God* whenever he can; that is, to blame God for the troubles of the world. Indeed, this is a very popular line of thinking nowadays—to blame God, the Bible, and Christians for all evils in the world—the state, the church, society, government, war, education, entertainment, etc. I am saying that the devil is totally behind this line of thinking and will exploit it no end.

Satan's job description therefore is not limited merely to his accusing us; he wants to accuse God. But *he does this through people*, to put evil thoughts into our heads in order to lure us into accusing God. So whenever we accuse God, we have mirrored the devil's own intent. It shows, sadly, that Satan has succeeded with us. I hate the thought that I would be part of Satan's conspiracy in the world to make God look bad. My job is to make God look good and totally wonderful. *Because He is.* But when I start to have bad thoughts about God, I am bordering on giving Satan his greatest pleasure. This is something I certainly don't want to do.

Secondly, Satan is God's tool for evil in this world. Why? You tell me. To inquire very long here, however, is to tiptoe into a place where angels fear to tread—the origin of evil, about which the Bible says little or nothing. You will recall that not knowing why God allows evil and suffering is what makes room for faith, so I refuse to be captivated by unprofitable speculation.

JOB

But one thing I can do is to draw your attention to the Book of Job. In it we learn many things, three of which are these:

1. Job—who lost his health, possessions, and reputation—never knew what was going on behind the scenes, that is, what was taking place in the spiritual world.

2. God instigated the ordeal that Job was to go through.

3. All that the devil was allowed to do to Job was by God's permission.

It may surprise you, but one day the Lord said to Satan, "Have you considered my servant Job? There is no one on earth like him; he is blameless and upright, a man who fears God and shuns evil" (Job 1:8).

In some ways this absolutely staggers me, that *God* would entice Satan to give Job a long era of evil and misery. In other ways, to be totally honest, this thrills me to my fingertips. I am so glad to know that all evil, hurt, injustice, and pain that has come upon me has—at least partly—a divine explanation: God Himself. I can live with this. In any case, it is for you and me to know and not forget: all trouble we endure in some sense starts with God. Don't ask me to explain this. I don't know any more than you do. I will add, however, the Book of Job ends as brilliantly and beautifully as it so inexplicably and strangely began. (See Job 1:8; 42:12.) Job never knew what was going on behind the scenes, but *we* know because we have the Book of Job.

Third, I bring the devil into my book to demonstrate we have a responsibility to keep Satan in proper perspective and to help people see the goodness of God. We must never—ever—forget that all that Satan does in this world is under the sovereign hand of God and by God's permission. Satan cannot move an inch without God allowing him to do so. As soon as the Lord brought Job to the devil's attention, Satan suggested to God that Job was happily serving Him only as long as Job prospered, was admired by everyone, and free from pain. So God gave Satan limited reign to bring pain and suffering on Job (Job 1:12).

The greatest sermon I ever heard was by Joseph Tson—preached at Westminster Chapel many years go. He spoke on mysterious reasons for suffering and took his text from the early verses in the Book of Job. He made a point I had never thought of: that one of the reasons we suffer is because the angels are watching us. The angels wanted to see what Job would do when unthinkable suffering came up on him. God let Job become a test case before the angels—who had never seen anything like this before—to see how Job would react. "The angels literally waited to see," said Joseph Tson, "what Job would do. God's honor was on the line before the angels." I find this deeply moving. If it brings God glory that the angels are watching to see whether I will still serve God when I am called to suffer, this is yet another good reason to be faithful.

Fourth, behind every negative thing that can emerge in one's life—whether it be a tragedy, illness, pain, disappointment, failure, loss, or financial reverse, you can be absolutely sure that Satan will exploit this to the hilt. His greatest pleasure is to make God look bad. He exists for this; it is what he loves to do.

Perhaps you have heard about Paul's thorn in the flesh (2 Cor. 12:7). Paul says God sent it to him lest he be exalted above measure (KJV), to keep from being conceited (NIV), or from being too elated (RSV). We have no idea what his thorn was, whether it was an illness, eye disease, an enemy, persecution, hard lifestyle, loneliness, handicap, or whatever; it was certainly something very painful in his life. The word *thorn* comes from a word that is like a fishhook stuck into your skin, not life-threatening but very painful. And Paul tells us that both God and Satan were at the bottom of it; the thorn was a messenger of Satan. Paul admits that he prayed unsuccessfully (three times) for it to go away. The only reply he got back from God was: "My grace is sufficient for you, for my power is made perfect in weakness" (2 Cor. 12:7–9).

So with us. Whether it be a thorn in the flesh or any kind of satanic attack, God's grace is sufficient to carry us through—however long it lasts. I pray you will see God as your loving Father who permitted it; also see Satan as your enemy who will try to make your life as miserable as possible. His job is to multiply the intensity, making us feel that it is either God's fault or our fault—a punishment for something we have done.

Fifth, as Job could not have known that behind all that was happening to him had originated in the spiritual world, so too our perception of what is so often going on in our lives. In a time of panic we may ask, "Whatever is going on? Why? Why now?" We may not have realized that behind our suffering, perplexities, and anger is the work of the devil. True, Satan only proceeds as far as God lets him—for the devil is *always* under God's thumb, and yet we may not have reckoned that what is going on in our lives has its origin behind the scenes in the spiritual world. The spiritual world is the realm in which Satan and all demonic forces thrive. This realm is *Tartarus*—the Greek word usually translated "hell," as in 2 Peter 2:4. It is *not* a reference to hell as a place of future punishment but only a word used to depict where evil powers reign.

Sixth, I have brought the subject of Satan into my book that you might know why your anger, irritability, or annoyance toward God may be intensified, that you will see the devil as being the explanation. As Job could not have known what was going on in the spiritual world—his life being in total misery for a while—so we should consider this dimension as an explanation of what is going on as well, to help us see why we feel so strongly negative at times.

God indeed gives the evil one permission to do what he does. Why? I don't know. But it is comforting that God is in control and that the devil is under God's sovereign hand. To put it another way, there is an architectural plan that lies behind what is happening in our lives. God has the first word and also the last word. Our job is to keep calm when hard, cruel, unfair, difficult, and negative things happen. All satanic attacks are temporary; that is, they last for a season. After Jesus's temptation was over, Satan left Jesus for a season (Luke 4:13, kjv). He may return later but only for a limited time. God knows how much we can bear. "No temptation [Greek *peirasmos*—trial or testing] has seized you except what is common to man. And God is faithful; he will not let you be tempted beyond what you can bear. But when you are tempted, he will also provide a way out so that you can stand up under it" (1 Cor. 10:13).

When the heat is on, then, we need to *stand*. The classic New Testament passage regarding spiritual warfare is Ephesians 6:10–18. Paul calls it a "day of evil." This does not necessarily mean a literal twenty-four-hour day but a time or season. The day of evil is when God gives the OK sign to Satan to attack us. Paul tells us how to react in such a day. Four times he uses the word *stand*. "Put on the full armor of God, so that you can take your *stand*...so that when the day of evil comes, you may be able to *stand* your ground, and after you have done everything, to *stand*. *Stand* firm then..." (Eph. 6:12–14, emphasis added). Why stand? It means you must not slip and fall, go backward—or even try to run ahead! All you and I are required to do when the evil day comes is to stand. You make great spiritual progress merely by *standing*. When the storm passes by—and it will—you will be stronger than you were before.

SATAN HATES GOD

In case you did not know, I have to tell you how much Satan hates the God of the Bible and His Son, Jesus Christ. There is no way to put into words how much Satan hates God, Jesus, and the Holy Spirit—and the church and Christians. His icy hatred toward those of us who have sided with his archenemy, Jesus Christ, cannot be calculated. If you are a Christian, you are his target. He will work overtime to bring you down, accusing you day and night (Rev. 12:10), which means he is at work when you are asleep.

However, it is also true that Satan hates everybody in the world—even in their preconversion state. He is known as the god of this age ("god of this world" [ESV]—2 Cor. 4:4). My dad used to say to me again and again, "Son, the devil is very crafty, and he is second only to God in wisdom and power." This is true. God has ultimate power, but Satan is second. True, a far second—way down in comparison. I think some people believe Satan has as much if not more power than God by the way they mention him all the time. But we need to get this straight: he is second to God in wisdom and power, but God is supreme and is in total control. Some Christians seem to think that there is a huge duel going on between good and evil—and are holding their breath to see who wins. No.

As I said, Satan could not touch us except by God's sovereign permission (Job 1). This is so encouraging. Please do not forget therefore that whenever you are being tempted or attacked by Satan that God allowed it—willingly and consciously. This means that Satan's attacks on us have passed through God's filtering test. God our heavenly Father loves us with an everlasting love; we are bought with a price, and He loves us infinitely more deeply than Satan hates us. God knows each of us by name and knows us intimately— backward and forward. He knows how strong we are, how weak we are, how mature we are, how shallow we are. He therefore calculates what we can bear before He lets Satan move in on our territory. This should encourage all of us. It certainly encourages me.

But one of my main points in writing this chapter is for you the reader to be aware that Satan will come alongside to *intensify* your negative thoughts. When something bad happens to you, the devil will not be looking the other way. In fact, he is working overtime—day and night as we saw before—to seize upon something bad that has happened to you in order to make God look bad and to make you want to accuse God. In a word: *be aware* of his tactics.

THE THREE RS OF
SPIRITUAL WARFARE

The apostle Paul made an interesting comment in this matter: "We are not unaware of his schemes" ("we are not ignorant of his devices"—2 Cor. 2:11, kjv). I say this guardedly, but it is a sign of considerable maturity to be able to recognize the devil when it is the *devil* and refuse to listen to him and resist him. The three Rs of spiritual warfare are: recognize, refuse, and resist. We need to know enough about the devil's ways to be able to say in adequate time this is the devil. But we need simultaneously to learn *not to listen to him*. As soon as you know it is your enemy, the devil, molesting you, *refuse to listen*. Then resist him. Remember: the devil is resistible. "Resist the devil, and he will flee from you" (James 4:7). It is true! But it begins with recognizing him and then refusing to listen to him.

When evil thoughts disturb us, we must turn him off—like pushing the delete button on a computer. Absolutely refuse to entertain or dwell on an evil thought. This would be true whether it is holding a grudge, dwelling on what someone has done to you, concentrating on the negative, feeling sorry for yourself, or blaming God for everything that has happened to you if it is unpleasant.

THE LAST THING THE
DEVIL WANTS YOU TO DO

The last thing in the world the devil wants you to do is to forgive God. He doesn't want you to let God off the hook! As long as you are pointing a finger to God and saying, "God, I hate You for this," you are making the devil's day. He is thrilled to no end when you speak to God like that.

Never forget that the devil is your enemy. He is no friend. He may slip alongside you and try to convince you he is your friend. This is why it is important to be able to recognize him—discern him and know his ways. One of the things Satan will do is to get you to focus on what you think is your right to be bitter. This is a dangerous thing to do! As Paul put it, a further reason to forgive is to keep from being outsmarted by Satan (2 Cor. 2:11). The devil will look for any possibility of getting an upper hand in your life. Be self-controlled and alert. "Your *enemy the devil* prowls around like a roaring lion looking for someone to devour. Resist him, standing firm in the faith, because you know that your brothers throughout the world are undergoing the same kind of sufferings" (1 Pet. 5:8–9, emphasis added).

SOME CHARACTERISTICS
OF SATAN

The devil is the tempter. He knows your ways backward and forward. He knows your personality. He knows your weaknesses. He will appeal to these. The variety of temptations are, for example:

1. Tempt you to doubt. Jesus was led by the Spirit into the desert to be tempted by the devil. The first thing the devil—called the tempter—did was to try to get Jesus to doubt. "The tempter came to him and said, 'If you are the Son of God, tell these stones to become bread'" (Matt. 4:3). The devil's tactic was to make Jesus question whether He truly was the Son of God. You just may not be the Son of God after all, Satan was suggesting. That said, it is not always sinful to doubt. Even John the Baptist questioned if Jesus really was the Messiah having already been told that He was, and Jesus commended him (Matt. 11:1–6).

2. Tempt you to confusion. When the serpent tempted Eve in the Garden of Eden, he immediately tried to get her to doubt the Word of God. "Did God really say, 'You must not eat from any tree in the garden'?", attempting to sow doubt (Gen. 3:1). Embedded in this suggestion

was also a distortion of what God actually said. God did not say that Adam and Eve could not eat of any tree, for they could indeed eat of any tree but one—called the tree of the knowledge of good and evil (Gen. 2:16–17). Satan wanted to confuse her as well as to get her to doubt.

3. Tempt you regarding physical needs. Satan also touched on Jesus's physical needs and wants. Jesus would have been hungry, having been fasting for forty days (Matt. 4:2). Hence the suggestion: "Tell these stones to become bread" (v. 3). Jesus was tempted at all points just like us but without sin (Heb. 4:15).

4. Tempt you to do something ridiculous. The devil took Jesus to the highest point of the temple in Jerusalem and told Him, if He was truly the Son of God, "Throw yourself down"—jump off! After all, said Satan—quoting Scripture: "He [God] will command his angels concerning you, and they will lift you up in their hands, so that you will not strike your foot against a stone'" (Matt. 4:5–6). The devil wants to make a fool of you! He will, if he can, persuade you to do something stupid and counterproductive. When Satan quotes Scripture I am reminded of William Perkins's comment: "Don't believe the devil, even when he tells the truth!"

5. Tempt you to pride. Satan led Jesus to a very high mountain and showed Him all the kingdoms of the world and their splendor. "All this I will give you," he said, "if you will bow down and worship me" (Matt. 4:9). The devil appealed to Jesus's self-esteem and suggested that He could have the whole world at His feet if He would worship Satan. It was an absolute lie, of course, but in Jesus's weakened state (from fasting forty days) the devil hoped that Jesus would be thrown off guard by this suggestion.

Satan is a liar. Jesus said of the devil, "There is no truth in him. When he lies, he speaks his native language, for he is a liar and the father of lies" (John 8:44). When Eve reminded the serpent that God said she would die if she ate of the tree of the knowledge of good and evil, Satan countered, "You will not surely die" (Gen. 3:4). The devil is inherently a liar and will do all he can to lure us to do the opposite of what God wills for us. One of the ways to know God's will is to figure out what you *think* the devil would want you to do—then do the opposite.

Satan is a deceiver. He even raises up false apostles, deceitful people who enter the Christian ministry, who masquerade as being true and solid. But "Satan himself masquerades as an angel of light. It is not surprising, then, if his servants masquerade as servants of righteousness" (2 Cor. 11:14–15).

If one does not have sufficient knowledge of Scripture and of the devil's ways, that man or woman can be shaken and taken in by those, especially on television, who deceive some of the best of God's people, exploiting their lack of sound biblical and theological knowledge, appealing to their greed and pride.

The devil is a bully. Peter likened Satan to "a roaring lion looking for someone to devour" (1 Pet. 5:8). Did you ever hear the roar of a lion? I have. Wow. What an awesome *sound*. The only lion I had ever heard roar was at the beginning of a MGM movie—until I was taken to a park in South Africa. I was not prepared for the volume and quality of the lion's roar. But what the roar often does is make its prey think the poor critter is already finished; he might as well give up now! Wrong. The roar is a bullying tactic to make you fear you have already been defeated. Remember, a lion can roar only when it has nothing in its mouth! It is another example of deceit.

Satan blinds. He is called the god of this world, or age. His job description in this regard is to blind us. He keeps us from seeing our sin, making us think we are decent, good, respectable, and fairly righteous people. He will help us to feel quite able in ourselves. When asked, "If you were to stand before God (and you will) and He were to ask you (and He might), 'Why should I let you into My heaven?'", what would you say? A lost person will usually say, "I have been a good person" (or something like that). This proves the person is blind. Satan's task particularly is to keep the lost person *lost*. Our gospel is "hid to them that are lost" (2 Cor. 4:3, KJV). After all, we are *all* born unsaved. No one is saved by birth, whether he or she has the best of parents, nor are they saved by baptism. To keep a person in a lost state is to blind him or her to the knowledge of the gospel "so they cannot see the light of the gospel of the glory of Christ who is the image of God" (2 Cor. 4:4). Satan's task is to keep a person from seeing the need for *faith*.

The devil is the great accuser. His job description in Revelation 12:10 is accuser of the brothers (and sisters of course). As we saw earlier in this chapter, the devil—who knows our past better than we know ourselves—will bring things to our attention that we have forgotten about. The purpose of this is to bring us down, to feel we are inadequate, not pleasing God, or are unsaved. He reminds us of our sins. That he works day and night is why we not only have bad dreams sometimes but also are awakened in the middle of the night—being suddenly reminded of things we and others have done—in order to rob us of sleep. He loves to do this. If he can keep us from sleeping, it makes his job easier during the day. He loves to strike *where* we are weak and *when* we are weak; e.g., when we have not slept well.

And, as I said, he delights in accusing God, coming alongside us to help us feel sorry for ourselves and blame God for all the evil He has permitted.

Satan knows his time is short. His doom is predestined: he will one day be thrown into the lake of burning sulfur to be tormented day and night forever and ever (Rev. 20:10). Whether he knew precisely what his punishment would be before this scripture was written in Revelation, or how he knows his time is short, I do not know. But the demons know they are not here indefinitely. When Jesus came upon demon-possessed men, the demons shouted to Him, "Have you come here to torture us before the appointed time?" (Matt. 8:29). The passage in Revelation speaks of the devil's great ire because he knows that his time is short (Rev. 12:12). So the next time the devil reminds you of your past, remind him of his future!

OVERCOMING SATAN

The good thing to realize in this brief and limited overview of the enemy is that he is resistible. He is not infinite. He is not all-powerful or all-knowing. I worry that some Christians fear the devil more than they do God. You need a healthy awareness for the devil, but do not fear him. He is under our sovereign and omnipotent God. He cannot move an inch without God's permission.

However, God has given Satan a measure of authority,

including the aforementioned characteristics. And the main thing Satan wants to do is to turn us against God. His greatest delight is making God look bad. He lives for that. The reason for this chapter is to make you aware of this.

I write this section also to show how to overcome him. The reason this is important is because you will excel by leaps and bounds in your Christian growth if you learn how to overcome Satan. In learning this, you are able also to appreciate, reverence, and love God—including totally forgiving Him for the things He has allowed that have possibly perplexed you. One of the best ways of all to overcome Satan is to forgive God—totally.

Resisting temptation. Jesus quoted Scripture to the devil with reference to His temptation to being hungry, "'Man does not live on bread alone, but on every word that comes from the mouth of God'" (Matt. 4:4). We do not know whether sexual temptation came during the time immediately after His forty day fast (it could have), but remember this: never blame God for temptation. It is easy to do. James realized this and said, "When tempted, no one should say, 'God is tempting me.' For God cannot be tempted by evil, nor does he tempt anyone; but each one is tempted when, by his own evil desire, he is dragged away and enticed" (James 1:13–14).

The temptation to do something ridiculous—such as jumping off a cliff and expecting God to hold you up and keep you from falling—can always be met with Jesus's reference to Deuteronomy 6:16: "Do not put the Lord your God to the test" (Matt. 4:7). Not looking after yourself by eating the wrong and unhealthy foods, not getting enough sleep, not taking care of your body, walking right into temptation deliberately, or handling money with carelessness—these examples relate to common sense. Not being careful in this area is tempting God. *Don't ever do that.* The devil will take full advantage of us when we put God to the test like that.

Temptation to pride is unavoidable in this life. We are all sinners and are vulnerable to taking ourselves too seriously, wanting the credit for every good thing we do, wanting to be admired, or needing the approval of people around us. But to the degree we are conscious of our weakness in this area, we can also anticipate how the devil will attack us and how we can anticipate such an attack and avoid it.

There is, of course, much more that could be said in this chapter about the devil. I only wanted to alert you to see how the devil will exploit our hurts and disappointments in order to make us *doubly* angry with God. And to the degree we are acquainted with Satan's ways—and not surprised when he shows up—we develop character and strength to overcome him when he does what he does best—to make the God of the Bible look bad. God is not bad; He is infinitely good (Ps. 100:5).

CHAPTER EIGHT

Deceitful Hearts

The heart is deceitful above all things and beyond cure. Who can understand it?

—JEREMIAH 17:9

Beware of no man more than of yourself; we carry our worst enemies within us.

—CHARLES H. SPURGEON (1834–1892)

T HE PURPOSE OF this chapter is partly to show that the devil, in a sense, has a rather easy job when it comes to getting people to hate God. This is because our fallen state—into which all of us are born—predisposes us to a natural hatred toward God without the devil's help. We are, simply, born that way.

And yet even after we are converted, although we have the Holy Spirit (Rom. 8:9), we aren't perfect. "If we claim to be without sin, we deceive ourselves and the truth is not in us" (1 John 1:8). Until we are glorified—which comes after the Second Coming of Jesus—we have deceitful, incurable hearts (Jer. 17:9).

One of the most neglected teachings in the church, speaking generally, is that of the fallen state of humankind. We have been fed throughout our generation (and before) the idea that people are basically *good*. This indoctrination has come partly from the church, partly from psychologists, partly from moralists, and largely from people who like to say things like this without thinking it through. And where has it gotten us? Evil and fear throughout the world are rampant. The notion that people are basically good is fundamentally flawed. The better we think we are, the worse things get.

AUGUSTINE'S FOUR STAGES

St. Augustine, one of the great Latin fathers of the early church, taught that humankind can be understood in terms of four states:

- Stage One: *posse peccare*—able to sin. This is the way God created Adam and Eve before the Fall (before they sinned in the Garden of Eden, as in Genesis 3). This means we were endowed with free will when first created. We were created without sin but nonetheless made by our Creator with the possibility of sinning. Adam and Eve could choose to sin or choose not to sin. They chose to sin. Things were never the same again.

- Stage Two: *non posse non peccare*—not able not to sin. This is the way you and I were from birth. This is the result of our first parents' sin in the garden. Their offspring were born with natural depravity with not only a proneness to sin but also an inability *not* to sin. So with all human-kind after that. "Surely I was sinful at birth, sinful from the time my mother conceived me" (Ps. 51:5). Sinning was therefore inevitable. That is why you and I have in common the fact that we are sinners.

- Stage Three: *posse non peccare*—able not to sin. This refers to those who have been regenerated by the Holy Spirit. This does not imply sinless perfection or even the possibility of it but rather an ability to resist temptation by faith and the Holy Spirit. God gives one a new heart; not one that is perfect, but one sufficiently changed nonetheless that he or she can glorify God by a holy life.

- Stage Four: *non posse peccare*—not able to sin. This is glorification—when all the redeemed are in heaven and have new bodies and hearts incapable of rebelling against God. That is exactly the way it will be to those who have been regenerated, justified by faith, and truly converted by the Holy Spirit. Not only will God clear His name on the last day, but also all of the saved will be given bodies incapable of disease and hearts unable to sin.

The problem with the widespread perception about the so-called goodness of humankind is that it assumes that what Augustine calls stage one—as man was before the Fall—to be the natural condition of all people today. There is no concept of a Fall in the first place in the minds of most people, much less the view that we inherited a sinful nature from birth. The teaching that we are brought into this world in this fallen state by birth is therefore out of the question for most people today. This idea, sadly, does not remotely come into the picture. They want to believe that all humankind is basically good—like Adam and Eve were before the Fall.

I don't want to be unfair. I only wish to bring back the biblical teaching regarding man. But without a good understanding of the Bible we will be naïve and bewildered as to the reason the world is as it is. "The Christian is a person who is not surprised that the world is as it is; he expects it," said Dr. Martyn Lloyd-Jones. The truth is, adverse and dangerous conditions should never surprise us; if anything, we may marvel that things are not worse than they are.

COMMON GRACE

The reason that humankind *isn't* worse than it is can be explained by the historic teaching known as common grace. It comes from John Calvin's idea of special grace in nature— which means that there is a touch of God's grace in all people whether saved or not. This common grace doesn't save a person but nonetheless prevents men and women from being worse than they might be otherwise. Common grace (called that not because it is ordinary but because it is given commonly to all) is God's goodness to all humankind; it provides the reason the world is not topsy-turvy and is not worse than it is. It is why we have law, police, firemen, doctors, hospitals, and nurses; why we have jobs that bless and touch society, postmen, schools, and people who are called to service to help us all.

Therefore the teaching of man's post-fallen state does not imply that men and women are as bad as they *could* be, but why we are as bad as we are. It saves us from a gullible and superficial view about the nature of men and women. We are born sinners—by nature loving darkness rather than light, born with a tendency to do wrong rather than right (John 3:19). We don't need to teach a child to lie. We don't need to teach a child to be selfish—or to lose their temper! We are born that way.

"All have sinned and fall short of the glory of God," says

Paul (Rom. 3:23). I am not pointing a finger necessarily at *you*, dear reader, when I say I know this about you: you are a sinner. Because I am a sinner. As one put it, great as any, worse than many. That's me.

Two Kinds of People

There are basically two kinds of people in the world today: lost and saved. In other words, there are (1) those who are in their post-fallen state but not yet converted because they have not (so far) responded to the gospel of Jesus Christ, and (2) those who have been converted.

What is the difference between the two when it comes to accusing God for the bad that is in the world? Sometimes very little, I'm sorry to say. But there is this essential difference: the unconverted, according to St. Augustine, are unable not to sin—they love darkness instead of light—whereas Christians are able not to sin; they come into the light (John 3:19–20). Sometimes Christians make the angels blush, however, by their anger when God lets bad things happen to them. I am writing this book to help in this area.

But Christians know not only that there is a God but also that He is all-loving and all-powerful. All of us struggle in varying degrees with the evil and suffering He permits.

Christians aren't perfect. When Jesus gave us the Lord's Prayer, it included the petition, "Forgive us our trespasses as we forgive those who trespass against us." (See Matthew 6:12.) He gave us this because He knew we would all sin. And yet, because we are in Augustine's third stage—able not to sin—we need to humble ourselves, lower our voices, and seek God's face. He will answer. You will recall that Habakkuk had his complaints; God answered. He had still more complaints; God answered again. We may not always like God's answers, but He is still talking to us and wants us to trust Him, to rely on His faithfulness. For He will have the last word. How much better it is if we affirm Him as He is revealed in the Bible now!

The best Christian on earth (whoever that may be) is still struggling with a heart that is deceitful and wicked, as Jeremiah 17:9 put it. The heart is beyond cure; that is, it will remain imperfect until we are in heaven. Here below we struggle with all kinds of imperfections—pride, jealousy, doubt, anger, ambition, and temptations of all sorts. And so I love Charles Spurgeon's quote, that we should "Beware of no man more than of yourself; we carry our worst enemies *within us.*"[1]

JOB

We aren't finished with Job yet! You may recall that in our previous chapter Job was seen as "blameless and upright, a man who fears God and shuns evil" (Job 1:8). If that were the way Job *always* was, we would have to say there is a possibility for sinless perfection in this life. But that is not the way Job was seen sometime later after Satan and Job's friends had a go at him. Job did begin in a most admirable way, however. After initial attacks from Satan, Job replied, "'The LORD gave and the LORD has taken away; may the name of the LORD be praised.' In all this, Job did not sin by charging God with wrongdoing" (Job 1:21–22). When his wife told him to curse God and die, he replied: "You are talking like a foolish woman. Shall we accept good from God, and not trouble?" (Job 2:9–10).

So far, so good. But little by little Job's friends—or accusers—kept probing him as for the *reason* he suffered so terribly—with painful boils, losing his health and all he had, including his possessions and good reputation. The assumption of Job's accusers was that he *must* have committed some terrible secret sin that God was punishing him for. Job knew that he had not sinned like that, and we have every reason to believe him. But Job began to get bitter. Truly bitter. Filled with self-pity. He lost his temper. He began to manifest the most despicable self-righteousness and arrogance along the way so that he became obnoxious. Whereas Job's friends were never vindicated for their accusations regarding Job, poor Job came out battered, bruised, and worn but with so much false piety that nobody admired him or could help him. That is, until God stepped in to make Job see things he had not seen before. It took God Himself to make Job see himself as he truly was. So with all of us; unless the Holy Spirit shows us our sin, we will go on and on and on believing we are good!

FOUR THINGS JOB LEARNED

We all can learn at least four things from Job's experience, among them:

1. Job himself was a terrible sinner after all, even if he had not committed murder or adultery. Sin is in one's thoughts as well as his or her deeds. Self-righteousness is vile and heinous in God's sight. It also puts everybody else off. Everybody could see Job's pitiful state except Job himself.

2. Job finally saw that his heart was as deceitful and incurably wicked as anybody else's. "I am unworthy—how can I reply to you? I put my hand over my mouth," Job finally said to God (Job 40:4).

3. After God stepped in as He did, Job came up with possibly the greatest line in this entire Book of Job: *"I know that you can do all things; no plan of yours can be thwarted"* (Job 42:2, emphasis added). When a person breaks though the betrayal barrier—or persists in faith long

enough after feeling let down by God to any degree—they too will joyfully conclude: God is all-powerful and no purpose of His can be thwarted.

4. Things changed for Job when he got over his bitterness. After Job had prayed for his friends, interceding on behalf of the very people who brought out his bitterness, "the LORD made him prosperous again and gave him twice as much as he had before" (Job 42:9).

It is a truth that we all need to discover for ourselves, namely, that bitterness of any kind, self-righteousness, and self-pity get us nowhere. These traits are always counterproductive. Whether our bitterness is toward the government, our parents, leaders, enemies, fellow Christians, the church, or God, we are only hurting ourselves to stay like this.

One of the ironies of church history is that the greatest saints always saw themselves as the greatest sinners. Job finally came to see this of himself. Isaiah the prophet apparently had a good ministry for years and then—suddenly—was given a vision of the glory of the Lord. He saw himself as he had not seen himself before: "Woe to me!...I am ruined! For I am a man of unclean lips" (Isa. 6:5). Paul said it of himself: "Christ Jesus came into the world to save sinners—of whom I am the worst" (1 Tim. 1:15).

My own theological background basically taught that Christians can and must live above sin, that they could actually live without ever sinning. They defined sin as transgressing against the known law of God. What they meant by that was not committing the kind of outward sin that was patently obvious to anybody. The problem was that they also included things such as women not wearing makeup or jewelry and men not smoking or drinking or anybody going to a cinema. It was a very warped way of looking at sin and sanctification. It took me a long time to get over it.

The biblical doctrine of sanctification—to which we are all called (1 Thess. 4:3)—is the process by which we are more holy and more like Jesus. But it is never perfected in this life. As John said, "If we claim to be without sin, we deceive ourselves and the truth is not in us" (1 John 1:8). Sanctification is therefore by degrees and never perfected this side of heaven. It wasn't perfected for Paul: "Not that I have already obtained all this, or have already been made perfect, but I press on to take hold of that for which Christ Jesus took hold of me. Brothers, I do not consider myself yet to have taken hold of it. But one thing I do: Forgetting what is behind and straining toward what is ahead, I press on toward the goal to win the prize for which God has called me heavenward in Christ Jesus" (Phil. 3:12–14). But one day we will be

completely like Him. For "those he justified, he also glorified" (Rom. 8:30).

In the meantime we struggle. We may wrestle with God.
Jacob began a wrestling match one evening with a strange
enemy that pounced on him out of the blue. But before the
night was over, he perceived that he was wrestling with the
best Friend he could ever have and began to beg that this
Friend bless him: "I will not let you go unless you bless me"
(Gen. 32:26). Martin Luther said that we must know God as
an enemy before we can know Him as a friend. This is true.
But I would go further: sometimes even in the Christian life
God hides His face—as if He were not our friend—to get
our attention.

WAS PAUL PERFECT?

You might ask: Was not the apostle Paul the greatest
Christian that ever lived? Perhaps. But he was far from perfect. He called the high priest—who was dressed in a prescribed religious garb and fully in charge of Paul's trial—a
whitewashed wall. Those standing near Paul said, "You dare
to insult God's high priest?" Paul quickly claimed he did
not realize that this man was the high priest! Of course he
knew! Paul was caught out! Does this surprise you, that the
great apostle Paul was human?

Not only that, the same Paul who told us not to be anxious

about anything (Phil. 4:6) admitted with extraordinary vulnerability to a most shocking anxiety and weakness when he had been in a very worried state of mind. It was when he was looking for Titus, whom he needed to see desperately. He came to Troas looking for Titus. When Paul got to Troas, he couldn't find Titus and concluded he wasn't there. But he was unexpectedly given an open door to preach while he was in town. And yet Paul, incredibly, turned the opportunity down! Who would have believed that Paul would not jump at the chance to preach the gospel? But he was in such consternation because Titus wasn't there that he took off for Macedonia (2 Cor. 2:12–13). Amazing. But it must be said that it is to Paul's credit that he—and not someone else—would be the one to tell this story, thus making himself extraordinarily vulnerable to his critics had they wanted to use this against him. I suspect that most of us would not want to admit openly to such a frailty lest it hurt our reputation. I am quite sure that I would be too afraid to be so transparent.

We are all sinners. We have all fallen short. We have all failed. We have all had thoughts that we would not want revealed to the world. And many of us have had thoughts toward God that weren't very nice. The wonderful thing is, we have a High Priest—Jesus—not like the one who was going after Paul but one who sympathizes with us. Our

Lord Jesus doesn't rub our noses in it. He is not like that; sending us on a guilt trip is *not* one of His ways. We have instead a heavenly Father who knows our frame and remembers that we are dust (Ps. 103:14).

What to Do When You Have Sinned

Therefore, for those who are in Augustine's stage three—who have been truly converted—what are we to do when we have failed or fallen? I answer: *tell it to God*. There is good old 1 John 1:9—a verse we all need every day. It was, after all, primarily written to Christians: "If we confess our sins, he is faithful and just and will forgive us our sins and purify us from all unrighteousness." What a wonderful verse! God is not only faithful but also *just* when He cleanses us. This is because the blood of Jesus has totally satisfied the divine justice. Had Jesus not pacified God's wrath by His death on the cross, it would not have been just for God to do this; it would have been impossible.

There are two words I find helpful here, even if they are theological terms: *expiation*—what Jesus's blood does for *us*, washing away our sins; and *propitiation*—what His blood does for *God*, turning His wrath away because He has been satisfied. John then followed with this exhortation: "My little children, I am writing these things to you so that you may not sin." God wants His sons and daughters to exhibit lives of holiness. And yet John immediately added, "But if anyone does sin, we have an advocate with the Father, Jesus Christ the righteous. He is the *propitiation* for our sins" (1 John 2:1–2, esv). We may well blush because of our deceitful, incurable hearts; I know I do. And yet this will not change until we reach stage four—when we are not able to sin. Until then we must do our best to resist the flesh and the devil. But one day we will be changed—glorified (1 Cor. 15:51–52). In the meantime we have an advocate who ever lives to intercede for us (Heb. 7:25).

To summarize: those who are in stage two of Augustine's chart (not able not to sin) are certainly easy work for the devil. Those of us who are in stage three (able not to sin) have the Holy Spirit dwelling in us. This means we should surely give the devil a more difficult time when he tempts us to be angry with God. I pray this chapter might be an aid to help us to improve in this area so that the devil has a harder time with us. I want to give Satan a hard time. This would indicate that I am growing, that I am not where I was years ago.

When certain people were trying to cast out devils in Ephesus more than two thousand years ago through Jesus whom Paul preached, the demons answered, "Jesus I know, and I know about Paul, but *who are you?*" (Acts 19:13–15, emphasis added). The devil did not recognize these upstarts. My old friend Rolfe Barnard used to preach a sermon he called "The Man Who Was Known in Hell," namely Paul. Paul had given Satan such trouble that the entire demonic world was fully aware of the apostle Paul. Paul was a threat to the devil. Paul had a reputation in hell—*Tartarus*, that spiritual realm where the demonic powers inhabit. Rolfe concluded that most people are not known in hell; they don't give the devil any trouble at all.

"I want to be known in hell," said Rolfe. So do I.

PART FOUR

Letting God off the Hook

Job replied to the Lord: "I know that you can do all things; no plan of yours can be thwarted."

—JOB 42:1–2

Forgiveness is an act of the will, and the will can function regardless of the temperature of the heart.

—CORRIE TEN BOOM (1892–1983)

CHAPTER NINE

Why Forgive God?

If only for this life we have hope in Christ, we are to be pitied more than all men.

—1 CORINTHIANS 15:19

Aim at heaven and you will get earth thrown in. Aim at earth and you will get neither.

—C. S. LEWIS (1898–1963)

I N THIS CHAPTER I wish to give three reasons why we should forgive God, that is, letting Him totally off the hook, and show why it is in our interest to do so.

1. LIFE BEYOND THE GRAVE

I sometimes think that the most forgotten doctrine in the church today, speaking generally, is that of heaven and hell: that the saved are going to heaven and the lost are going to hell. This traditional teaching of the truth is either true— or it isn't. If there is neither heaven nor hell, there is no reason to forgive God. One of the chief reasons to forgive

God—that is, to let Him totally off the hook for the evil He has allowed in this world and in our lives—is because eternity follows the last day—when God will clear His name.

Another way of putting it, there will be two classes of people at the final judgment: those who will be glad they cleared God's name in advance of that day and those who will wish they had done so. By clearing God's name I simply mean that you totally forgive Him for all He has permitted that is evil. It means you let Him off the hook—and never look back.

I now speak to a somewhat popular notion that you hear from some Christians: *If there were no heaven and no hell, I would still be a Christian.* I know what people mean by that. Their lives have changed and they are happier because they have relied on Jesus's death to forgive them for their sins. Not only that, but also to overcome bitterness and to become a thankful person is healthy. Medical people tell us that holding a grudge is injurious to your health. Unforgiveness can lead to maladies such as heart disease, high blood pressure, kidney disease, and arthritis. Medical science has also determined that people who are thankful live longer!

So there are some fairly good *earthly* reasons for being a Christian and following Jesus's teaching about forgiveness and being grateful.

But tell that to the apostle Paul! Does it surprise you that Paul says what he does: "If only for this life we have hope in

Christ ["being a Christian"—TLB], we are to be pitied more than all men" (1 Cor. 15:19). Paul is saying to us that it would be utterly foolish for him to be a Christian if there were no heaven to look forward to one day. Listen to him: "We go hungry and thirsty, we are in rags, we are brutally treated, we are homeless. We work hard with our own hands. When we are cursed, we bless; when we are persecuted, we endure it; when we are slandered, we answer kindly. Up to this moment we have become the scum of the earth, the refuse of the world" (1 Cor. 4:11–13). There is more:

> I have...been in prison more frequently, been flogged more severely, and been exposed to death again and again. Five times I received from the Jews the forty lashes minus one. Three times I was beaten with rods, once I was stoned, three times I was shipwrecked, I spent a night and a day in the open sea, I have been constantly on the move. I have been in danger from rivers, in dangers from bandits, in danger from my own countrymen, in danger from Gentiles; in danger in the city, in danger in the country, in danger at sea; and in danger from false brothers. I have labored and toiled and have often gone without sleep; I have known hunger and thirst and often gone without food; I have been cold and naked.
>
> —2 CORINTHIANS 11:23–27

So if you could tell Paul one should be a Christian if there were no heaven to look forward to, he would answer: "You must be stupid. You must be joking! We are utter fools to uphold the Christian faith if it is all about living on this earth."

And yet it would be a mistake to conclude that Paul only said what he did because he had suffered so much. That would miss the point. He made this throwaway comment because he was affirming Jesus's resurrection from the dead. He was arguing that the reason Jesus was raised from the dead is because we too will be raised from the dead. The proof of our future resurrection is Jesus's resurrection. It would not happen had He not been raised. Therefore to make too much about the good things that might come to a Christian in this life would miss the reason Jesus died and rose from the dead.

My point is this. Christianity is a supernatural religion. We affirm that Jesus literally rose from the dead—in the same body (although it was transformed). The point of the empty tomb on Easter was that it was the same Jesus who died who also was resurrected. His glorified body could walk through doors (John 20:19). So though it was the same body, it was a glorified body.

So too with you and me. These very bodies of ours will be raised one day. We look forward to that day when we see Jesus face-to-face. Even Jesus Himself looked forward to the joy that was set before Him. He certainly did not enjoy suffering for our sins. There was nothing pleasant about it. He endured the cross, "scorning its shame" (Heb. 12:2), "despising the shame" (ESV, KJV). He hated it.

So if you believe Paul, you will not adopt the view that the Christian faith is still worth upholding if there is no life beyond the grave. "Nonsense," says Paul. Rubbish. Total absurdity. Silly thinking.

The truth is, however, that "Christ *has indeed* been raised from the dead, the firstfruits of those who have fallen asleep [died]" (1 Cor. 15:20, emphasis added). Because He was raised we too shall be raised. Not only that, but we will also be present on that day when every knee shall bow and every tongue confess that Jesus Christ is Lord to the glory of God the Father (Phil. 2:9–11; Rom. 14:11). We who have cleared God's name in advance of that day will have front-row seats, as it were, rejoicing with immeasurable satisfaction. Being present when God vindicates Himself will vindicate our decision to let Him off the hook before He does it Himself—which, by the way, will remove the need for faith. For when God clears His name, it will be done in a manner that will remove all doubt. We might even say, "Why didn't we think of that?", when He reveals the ultimate reason for evil and suffering. In any case it will be clear and unmistakable.

Why should we forgive God? We will be so glad that we did.

2 . Developing Character

I will now make a case for being a Christian because of what it *can* do for you in this life. It is as C. S. Lewis said: "Aim for heaven and you get the earth thrown in. Aim at earth and you will get neither."[1] After all, we don't go straight to heaven as soon as we are converted! There is a life out there to be lived; some live fifty years, some sixty, some into their nineties. What manner of people are we to be like?

Job again

We have given some attention to Job. All the suffering he endured eventually led him to the conclusion that God is all-powerful and that no purpose of God can be *thwarted*—overthrown or defeated. He overcame his bitterness by forgiving his friends, even interceding for them. I realize that not all who have suffered with pain and unthinkable hurt have come through such suffering as Job did. I know some who remained bitter owing to what they went through and, if anything, were more bitter afterward. Some of these were known to be Christians, some of them high profile.

There is no merit in suffering per se. The only value of suffering is when God is welcomed into one's suffering. I think one possibly needs to make a decision sooner than later when bad things come along. Our first reaction may be panic and a temptation to be angry with God—which is so understandable; but if one cools off fairly early on in a trial, he or she can reap incalculable benefit. When you read the first two chapters of Job—when he seemed so triumphant and impressive—you have a picture of a total hero! He puts us all to shame. Then when you see the same Job under pressure when his friends were so cruel and unrelenting—and Job caves in—you wonder why we have those early chapters. We say to ourselves when reading them, "What value was it that Job praised God and rejected his wife's advice? He turns out to be human like all of us. What good was it that he said, 'Blessed be the name of the Lord,' and refused to charge God foolishly—when he was so bitter later on?"

I reply: Job's effort to dignify the trial arose from the strong character he truly was at that time the dam broke and the suffering set in. His honoring God as he had done wasn't for nothing. He had built up strength and discipline. So when trouble first emerged, he was sufficiently strong not to give in and panic. Furthermore, had Job cursed God, as his own wife advised, we would never have heard of Job. Neither would he have come out of it as he did.

This is another way of saying I am not sure *any* of us could withstand the treatment his friends gave him without being angry and defensive. That was part of the point of his suffering—that Job see what he was truly like underneath.

We are all like that. Given sufficient pressure, we too would show how self-righteous and full of pity we are.

But here's the thing: God was with Job in all this because Job was such a strong believer from the beginning. This is why we must all be faithful in the little things—when the smaller trials come. Jesus said, "He who is faithful in what is least is faithful also in much" (Luke 16:10, NKJV). So if you and I are maintaining lives of gratitude, faith, walking in the light, and totally forgiving our enemies, then we too will come through the worst of ordeals as Job did—even if our imperfections erupt in the meantime. Nobody's perfect.

3. Being Like Jesus

Every Christian is predestined to be like Jesus: "Those God foreknew he also predestined to be conformed to the likeness of his Son, that he might be the firstborn among many brothers" (Rom. 8:29). This is our glorious future—when we will have been changed to be like Him, for "we shall see him as he is" (1 John 3:2). In other words, it is only a matter of time when every single child of God will be just like Jesus. We will be utterly pure and without sin. It does not mean we will be God; Jesus will not have surrendered His deity to us. It means that we will have bodies that are free of any disease and hearts that are incapable of sinning.

However, the period between our justification by faith

and glorification is called sanctification—that process by which we are more and more like Jesus. Part of our purpose on earth as Christians is to develop character. It happened to Job; it should happen to all of us. Paul said that we even "rejoice in our sufferings, because we know that suffering produces perseverance; perseverance, character; and character, hope. And hope does not disappoint us, because God has poured out his love into our hearts by the Holy Spirit, whom he has given us" (Rom. 5:3–5).

Paul said, "It has been granted to you on behalf of Christ not only to believe on him, but also to suffer for him" (Phil. 1:29). That suffering may certainly be persecution, as it was to these Philippians. But what if it is a different kind of suffering? What if you live in a part of the world that is generally free of persecution? I happen to live in the Bible Belt of America—you could say that Nashville, Tennessee, is the buckle of that belt! I haven't heard of anybody lately that has been put in jail for their faith. I haven't heard of anyone being burned at the stake or threatened with death if they don't stop being Christian. Am I to believe that the only kind of suffering is persecution because you are a Christian? If so, some of us would never qualify for Christian suffering, if I may put it that way. Was Job's suffering for Christ?

My point is this. We should regard *any* suffering that comes to us as God's way for us to develop character. How we react to the suffering that is handed to us would indicate how we would handle extreme persecution. As I said, he or she who is faithful in what is least will be faithful in much (Luke 16:10). So if God allows suffering through sickness, death of a loved one, financial reverse, losing your job, marriage breakdown, withholding of vindication, or the most vile kind of pain, we should take this from God as a test to develop our character. We can be like Jesus, then, in *any* kind of suffering. It is a time to totally forgive those who have hurt us, a time to dignify the trial, to refuse to be bitter, and to turn the cheek as Jesus did.

Jesus lived a life of total forgiveness. There was not an ounce of bitterness in Him. He was tempted in every way but without ever sinning (Heb. 4:15). There were the smaller things He faced—such as sibling rivalry. His brothers were jealous of Him and taunted Him, saying He needed to be in Jerusalem to get His name known! No one who wants to become a public figure acts in secret (John 7:5), as if this sort of thing was important to Him! Or take the way He interacted with Sadducees and Pharisees—who were always looking for a chance to show Him up or bring Him down (Matt. 22:15–45). And when it came to His toughest hour—facing His death on the cross, "when they hurled their insults at him, he did not retaliate; when he suffered, he made no threats" (1 Pet. 2:23). He who did everything He ever did by following the Father's cue (John 5:19) never once said, "This is not fair. Why do You put Me with brothers like this? Why do You make Me listen to these Pharisees and Sadducees? Why did You let Pilate crucify Me?" No. Not once. "Instead, he entrusted himself to *him who judges justly* (1 Pet. 2:23, emphasis added).

There was one moment, however, when Jesus questioned His Father. It was on Good Friday when hanging on the cross. We will not know until we get to heaven—and I am not sure we will know then—what it was like when Jesus suffered on the cross. I am not referring now to the physical sufferings—the flogging, the nails in His hands, or the crown of thorns on His head; I refer to the worst suffering any human being ever—ever—suffered. It was when the Father apparently turned His back on Jesus. He cried out, "My God, my God, why have you forsaken me?" (Matt. 27:46). He felt utterly and totally deserted by the Father at the precise moment He suffered the most. I do not pretend to understand all this, but it was the very moment when all our sins were transferred from us to Him. The Lord laid on Him the iniquity of us all (Isa. 53:6). It was overwhelming. It was too much to bear. He could not endure it without questioning the Father. And yet we are told He never sinned (Heb. 4:15; 1 Pet. 2:22). That tells me it is OK to ask God why. It is not a sin to ask the reason why. God may not tell us in this life the very reason He allows us to suffer. But it is no sin to ask.

But remember one thing. No human being ever suffered as Jesus did. The next time you are tempted to be angry with God and question His integrity, remember Jesus. He did not question God's integrity. "He entrusted himself to him who judges justly" (1 Pet. 2:23). He only asked why.

We too can ask why and do so without sinning. But if we charge God with injustice and criminal activity because of what He lets us endure, we cross over a line—which would be sinning.

Why totally forgive God? Because the development of our character is at stake. The same people who tell us that holding a grudge can lead to physical problems also tell us that the greatest benefit of forgiveness is not to the one who gets forgiven but to the one who forgives. It was Alexander Pope (1688–1744) who said, "To err is human; to forgive, divine."[2] God calls on each of us—where this is our situation—to set God free and be rid of the bitterness. To do so is what makes us people of character, virtue, and strength. And we are becoming more and more like Jesus too—which honors God the Father more than anything we can ever do.

Paul may or may not have been the greatest Christian who ever lived. But almost certainly he accomplished more for the kingdom of God than any person who ever lived. He accomplished so much that it was hard to put any kind of goal before him that would excite him anymore. He came up with things such as preaching the gospel at Corinth without any remuneration (1 Cor. 9:18); he worked as a tentmaker to pay his bills. Another thing was that he only wanted to preach the gospel where no one had preached it before (Rom. 15:20). Extraordinary. Most ministers I know only want to go where there is already a foundation laid, that they can have a good, comfortable salary and maintain living in their comfort zone. Not Paul. In fact, if I have understood him correctly, he ended up with only one goal in life: "I want to know Christ and the power of his resurrection and the fellowship of sharing in his sufferings, becoming like him in his death" (Phil. 3:10). That is what he lived for. It was the only thing that excited him. But note: this included the fellowship of sharing in His sufferings. Whoever would want that? Paul did.

In other words, the same Paul who knew he was predestined to be like Jesus in any case wanted to get a head start (if I may put it that way) before going to glory. The way forward was to aim to be like Jesus. This meant bearing the cross and welcoming whatever suffering God laid on him.

The fringe benefit of this: one's character develops in great measure.

A REWARD AT THE
JUDGMENT SEAT OF CHRIST

What I present now in this book may have limited appeal to some. As I accept that there are those who have no need to break the betrayal barrier because they never felt betrayed by God in the first place, I accept that there are those who don't especially aspire to have a reward in heaven. There are those who say: "I just want to make to heaven; I don't have the slightest desire to have a reward in addition to being in heaven." I understand that.

However, with deepest respect, forgive me if I tell you that Paul would not agree with you. He not only looked forward to heaven, as we saw above, but he also wanted more! You may say, "How greedy!" But like it or not, a reward at the judgment seat of Christ was very, very important to him. He wanted that prize or crown. In fact, he wanted it so much that he said, "I beat my body and make it my slave also that after I have preached to others, I myself will not be disqualified for the prize" (1 Cor. 9:24–27).

Here, in a word, is Paul's teaching regarding this: all who are saved will go to heaven, but not all who go to heaven will receive a reward at the judgment seat of Christ. Some will be saved by fire. Let me explain. You and I who are justified by faith are set on a foundation—Jesus Christ. All who are saved are already on that foundation. But we have a responsibility to build a superstructure *on* that foundation (1 Cor. 3:10). In doing so there are two types of materials: those that cannot burn and those that can be burned up. The metaphors that Paul uses are gold, silver, and costly stones (which cannot burn), and wood, hay, or straw (which can be burned up). If we build a superstructure with what cannot burn up—gold, silver, and precious stones, we will receive a reward. If we build a superstructure of materials that can be burned up—wood, hay, or straw—we will not have a reward.

So on that day of days that we have been talking about in this book—the final day when the judgment seat of Christ will be unveiled—Paul says it will actually be revealed with fire (1 Cor. 3:13). The fire will test the quality of each person's superstructure. When the fire is applied to our superstructure, it will show what materials we used. The fire will test it. "If what he has built survives [because he built with gold, silver, costly stones], he will receive his reward" (1 Cor. 3:14). But "if it is burned up, he will suffer loss; he himself will be saved, but only as one escaping through the flames" (1 Cor. 3:15).

In other words the person whose works are burned up will *still* go to heaven, but he will have no reward. Works therefore do not determine whether one gets to heaven. We are saved by grace through faith alone, "not by works, so that no one can boast" (Eph. 2:9). However, said Paul, "we are God's workmanship, created in Christ Jesus to do good works, which God prepared in advance for us to do" (Eph. 2:10). Those who do these good works, then, will receive a reward for doing so at the judgment seat of Christ. This is why Paul said that "we must all appear before the judgment seat of Christ, that each one may receive what is due him for the things done while in the body, whether good or bad" (2 Cor. 5:10).

Like it or not, then, we must all stand before the judgment seat of Christ. We may or may not aspire *now* to have a reward at that time, but we will still stand before the righteous Judge and give an account of the things done while in the body, meaning the bodies we now have. I think we will wish then that a reward would be coming to us. I suspect that we will find that to be a scary, awesome time, although John talked about having boldness or confidence on the Day of Judgment (1 John 4:16). I doubt we can feel that way at the moment—except we can be confident now we will go to heaven. True, we can certainly know we are saved now— and therefore be confident. But as for receiving a reward, even Paul was not sure at one time whether he would receive a reward at the judgment seat of Christ. However, when death was at hand, he was sure of his reward. He said: "I have fought the good fight, I have finished the race, I have kept the faith. Now there is in store for me the *crown* of righteousness, which the Lord, the righteous Judge, will award to me on that day—and not only to me, but also to *all* who have longed for his appearing" (2 Tim. 4:7–8, emphasis added). This is a timely word to those of us who may think only the apostle Pauls of this world get a reward. Not true! It is for all of us who build our superstructures with gold, silver, and costly stones.

The question is, then, *what* gets us a reward? How do you know *you* are building a superstructure of gold, silver, and costly stones rather than wood, hay, or straw? The answer in part is whether we have totally forgiven those who have hurt us. Jesus even talked about a reward being great (Luke 6:35). But what determined that great reward? "Bless those who curse you, pray for those who mistreat you.... Love your enemies, do good to them... *then your reward will be great*" (Luke 6:27–28, 35, emphasis added). Jesus also said if people insult us, persecute us, and say all kind of evil against us because of Him, "great is your reward in heaven" (Matt. 5:11–12).

Total forgiveness means letting *everyone* who has hurt us in any way off the hook. *This includes God* if we feel He has hurt us by allowing what He did.

How do we erect a superstructure of wood, hay, or straw? I am sure this is partly done by living a life filled with bitterness, anger, and hurt over what has happened to us. We can choose to forgive or not to forgive. As Corrie ten Boom put it, "Forgiveness is an act of the will, but the will can function regardless of the temperature of the heart." What she meant by that is that we may not *feel* like forgiving those who have hurt us. You may not *feel* like forgiving God for what He has allowed that has hurt you so much. But if you equally know it is the right thing to do, I lovingly suggest to you: *choose to do it.* Don't wait until you feel like it. If you wait until you feel like it, chances are you will never do it. In other words, don't wait until you feel led, as if led by the Holy Spirit. The Holy Spirit would always lead you to do it because of what He has taught in the Word. He would not lead some to forgive and not lead others to do so. God is no respecter of persons; He loves us all equally. But if you make the choice to forgive—though you feel at that moment it is all in your own strength—in time you will *feel* it and see in retrospect that only the Holy Spirit could have enabled you to do what you did. Make the choice to forgive God completely, utterly, and totally, whether you feel like it or not. But eventually you will even feel like it—and find it easier and easier and easier to do. What is more, I guarantee it: *you will never be sorry.* On top of that there is a reward that will be waiting for you on that day of days.

As I said at the beginning of this chapter, there will be two sorts of people at the judgment seat of Christ: those who will be so glad they totally forgave God—by clearing His name in advance of that day—and those who will wish they had because they will see God's great vindication of Himself but will have forfeited the inestimable privilege of coming to that realization—without faith.

As of now there is still time for all of us to clear His name—by faith.

Which category will you be in?

CHAPTER TEN

How to Forgive
God—Totally

Do not be angry with yourselves for selling me here, because
it was to save lives that God sent me ahead of you. So then,
it was not you who sent me here, but God.

—GENESIS 45:5, 8

I'm a Christian because it's true.

—JONI EARECKSON TADA

I N MY BOOK *Total Forgiveness* I attempted to show how
to know that you have totally forgiven those who have
hurt you. In this connection I draw from the life of
Joseph, Jacob's favorite son, who totally forgave his brothers
for the evil they had done to him twenty-two years before.
They were so jealous of him that they were going to kill him.
But they decided to sell him to Ishmaelites who showed up
at the exact time they would have left Joseph in a pit to die.
A famine took place many years later, and the brothers had

to go to Egypt to purchase food. When the eleven brothers came to Egypt, they had to approach the prime minister, who was Joseph himself, but they did not know at first it was he. Joseph himself always knew that one day he would see them bowing down to him; it was given to him through prophetic dreams (Gen. 37:5–9). But he assumed those dreams were given to him so he could one day face those men and say "Gotcha!," watch them cower before his eyes, and then he could throw the book at them. But by the time the dreams were actually fulfilled, Joseph was a changed man; indeed a *new* Joseph had emerged. Instead of pointing the finger at them, he broke down, wept, and beautifully demonstrated that he had totally forgiven them.

The way Joseph forgave his brothers is a good way to know we have forgiven those who have hurt us. We can also learn from Joseph's example—to a degree—whether we have forgiven God.

Many people who have undergone deep suffering and trauma are not necessarily bitter toward God but simply fear that God doesn't love them because He allowed what He did. This applies to those who were born with a handicap or who have had terrible things happen to them in life. "Why would God do this if He loved me?" they ask. "Why was I born unattractive?" "Why do I not have a brilliant mind?" "Why did God allow me to marry the wrong person?" "Why did I not get to go to college?" "I have friends who get to go to university and get married, so does God love them more than He loves me?"

We all still need to let God off the hook for these things. It is often hard to feel that He loves us when these things happen to us. What are we to do? I believe we must *choose to believe the truth* of what He says in His Word. I would urge you not to measure His love for you by how well off you are or to assume He does not love you because of what evil things have taken place. Accept what He says about Himself in His Word. We may not *feel* it, but we *are* loved with an everlasting love (Jer. 31:3). It is the Holy Spirit who will give us the inner testimony that the Bible is true. We rely on the love God has for us (1 John 4:16). "We love because he first loved us" (v. 19).

You may recall that when Joni Eareckson Tada was a teenager, she was paralyzed from the neck down owing to a diving accident. For forty-five years now she has been a quadriplegic. She has probably had hundreds and hundreds pray for her healing—from the anointing of oil to laying on of hands. She has lived these years with a robust faith in God and His sovereignty and has a cheerfulness and smile on her face that put many of us to shame. But the most profound thing I ever heard her say was that she did not believe in Christianity because of what it *did* for her but because it is true.

This is the point to which we must all come—to believe the Bible because it is true and not necessarily for what God does for us. Equally we should not mistrust Him because of what He lets happen to us. What honors Him most is our confidence in His Word—even though we don't get all our questions answered.

How to Know We Have Forgiven God

We must be careful how we talk about God who allowed bad things to happen to us. Although I completely understand it when people say, "God must not love me because so many negative things have happened." Or some ask, "What have I done wrong that these things have happened to me?" You may recall that Job's so-called friends were convinced that he had done something terrible or God would not have let bad things happen to him. *They were completely wrong.*

Once you have truly and totally let God off the hook for what He allowed in your life, you should not keep saying that God must not love you or blame yourself because certain things have happened to you. The danger is that one can become bitter. Giving into bitter feelings will not cause the bitterness to go away. Like looking at pornography, the more one indulges in it, the more one needs still more of it. In much the same way venting one's bitterness or self-pity only causes you to get stirred up all the more. When we have been angry with God—but have forgiven Him—the first step is to guard our lips when we talk about God.

Tell God that you love Him. When Joseph's brothers suddenly realized that the prime minister of Egypt was their brother to whom they had done this terrible deed, they were terrified (Gen. 45:3). Joseph did not want them to feel that way; he wanted to embrace them. "Come close to me," he pleaded with them (v. 4). Joseph was a completely different person from what he once was. Telling God that you love Him may be the hardest thing you have ever had to do in your life. "But perfect love casts out fear" (1 John 4:18, NKJV), and when you perceive it is something He wants to hear from you, just maybe you will tell Him that you love Him.

This must not be a feigned love. Whereas the decision to forgive is an act of the will—regardless of how you *feel*—love can be a genuine feeling. However, a case can be made that love is what you *do* rather than what you feel. Yes. And we must sometimes begin with *doing* rather than *feeling*. But what Joseph was doing in saying to his brothers, "Come close to me," sprang from his true affection for them. As soon as you are able to do so, tell God that you love Him. He wants to hear it from you. Perhaps tomorrow it will be easier than today. Keep it up. God is not offended that you are struggling in this area. He knows what we are like inside and out, never forgetting that we are dust (Ps. 103:14).

Set God free by overcoming self-pity. Joseph told his brothers not to be distressed or angry with themselves because of the evil they did (Gen. 45:5). This is remarkable; he refused to let them feel guilty. Most of us cannot forgive very easily until the people who hurt us are *sorry* for what they did. It takes minimal grace to forgive a person if they are sorry; it takes maximum grace to forgive when they are not the slightest bit repentant. Jesus should be our model; He prayed for those who crucified Him when these men were not the slightest bit sorry for what they did. "Father, forgive them, for they do not know what they are doing" (Luke 23:34). We, however, naturally want to see their being sorry for what they did to us. This is partly because we are feeling sorry for ourselves that we had to be put through what they did to us. It is our self-pity that is a driving force in wanting our enemy to feel sorry; we want them to feel pity toward *us*! Joseph, however, was emptied of self-pity and set his brothers totally free—"Do not be angry with yourselves."

As I have said, self-pity gets us nowhere with God. Absolutely nowhere. As James put it, our wrath does not work the righteousness of God (James 1:20, KJV). We may wish that our sulking and hurt might move God to feel pity for us. I'm sorry, but it doesn't work that way. As long as we are feeling sorry for ourselves and are hoping this will make God sorry for what He allowed in our lives, dream on! I wish it weren't so! But self-pity does not make God say, "I'm so sorry for allowing you to go through this," as if He owes us an apology. Self-pity is our unsubtle attempt to manipulate God. He doesn't fall for it. As Joseph refused to let his brothers feel distress over what they did, so we too must set God totally free by refusing to make Him feel He has wronged us. Don't go there. Don't even think it!

Affirm God's greater purpose He had in mind when He allowed you to suffer. It is only a matter of time when you will see that God permitted what He did in your life because He had a purpose in it. It was not for nothing. It was not an accident. You have not been existentially thrown into your existence without meaning. God created you and is the ruler over all. A leaf falls from a tree by His hand. He feeds the sparrows. He clothes the earth with beauty. He knows how many hairs are on your head. Whatever has happened to you was not when He had His head turned. He was looking straight at you.

I am sure Joseph was filled with self-pity and anger for a long time. He needed time to do what he did. Total forgiveness is not easy. "Broken wings take time to mend,"[1] as my friend the late Janny Grein put it in one of her songs. Joseph needed time to come to terms with God and His allowing what He did in letting him suffer so much.

By stating it as he did to his brothers—*what you did is really what God did*—Joseph shows in bold relief that he had not only forgiven them but had also *totally forgiven God*. Joseph assured his brothers that it was actually God who was at the bottom of what they did twenty-two years before. Therefore it wasn't what they did but what God did. Amazing! I call it saving face; Joseph let his brothers save face. Instead of making them look bad, he made them feel good and made God look good, God being the architect of the entire matter. This way his brothers should not feel guilty. Instead of rubbing their noses in it, then, Joseph demonstrated that it was God who orchestrated the whole thing. "It was not you who sent me here [by your selling me to the Ishmaelites], but God" (Gen. 45:8). Joseph is actually saying that the evil his brothers did—first, planning to kill him but then deciding to sell him to the Ishmaelites—was what God Himself was doing.

Totally forgiving God is what you will have to do for the rest of your life. I call it a life sentence. As a physician may give a patient a tablet, telling them, "You will have to take this for the rest of your life," so it is with total forgiveness. In the case of Joseph, he demonstrated that he kept it up. Seventeen years later old Jacob died. The eleven brothers assumed that Joseph was only waiting for their father to die so he could at last get vengeance upon them. They made up a story. They came running to Joseph to say, "Dad told us to tell you please to forgive us for what we did to you." Joseph starts to cry. He can't believe his brothers! He therefore had to reassure them as if to say, "I forgave you seventeen years ago; I forgave you then and I forgive you now." (See Genesis 50:15–19). The genius of Joseph was that he *really had forgiven them.* The point is, it still held good after seventeen years.

It is not enough to say once to God: *"I let You off the hook; I do forgive You."* You may have to do it again tomorrow. Next week. Next year. Ten years from now. It is a life commitment, a life sentence; to show you meant it, you do it on and on and on. The devil will do all he can to remind you of the evil things done to you—and try to make you bitter toward God all over again. Don't listen to him. Remember the three Rs of spiritual warfare: recognize, refuse, resist. Do not be surprised that your enemy the devil will remind you of the evil that came upon you—to make you angry with God. Recognize Satan, refuse to listen to him, resist him—and he will flee from you.

Bless the Lord for all He has done in your life. Joseph assured his brothers that they would be looked after. He blessed them, assured them that they would be provided for. Jesus told us to bless our enemies (Luke 6:27–28). You may recall that when Job was first hit by horrible suffering, he graciously said, "The Lord gave and the Lord has taken away;

may the name of the LORD be praised" (Job 1:21). If only Job had maintained that position!

Perhaps you felt God was like an enemy when He first allowed you to go through unthinkable disappointment and suffering—when He could so easily have stopped it. But He didn't. He let you go through deep, deep hurt. But given sufficient time you saw that He was with you after all. It is like that account (seen earlier) when Jacob wrestled with an enemy only to realize it was a wonderful friend—and begged to be blessed. I am saying to you: bless the Lord who seemed like your enemy. The sooner you can praise the Lord—as if like blessing your enemy—the better. The day will come that it won't be an effort to do it. It will be easier and easier and easier.

FIVE SUGGESTIONS

Overcoming hurts through total forgiveness is one of the most difficult things in the world to do. It is arguably the most major challenge one can accept in this life. I therefore put the following suggestions *not* as easy steps but rather as things for you to consider as a way forward in setting God free (if you have not done so).

1. Be totally honest with God and tell Him your complaint.

David said, "I pour out my complaint before him; before him I tell my trouble" (Ps. 142:2). This means to tell God but not the world. Perhaps you have heard of the old spiritual that came out of the Deep South in the nineteenth century. It came out of the cotton fields from black slaves who were so rudely and wickedly treated: "Nobody knows the troubles I've seen; nobody knows but Jesus."

The truth is, God likes it when He is the only one who knows! We all need someone to share our griefs with—thank God for friends. But when the Lord alone knows what you have been through—and no one else—you are letting Him in your feelings and not others. When a friend confides in you and you know you are the only one who knows what he or she has been through, you are affirmed in a significant way. God wants to have that place in your life—when He is the only one you tell. It has given me great consolation over the years when I was tempted to tell this person or that one what I have been through to hear the Lord saying, "RT, *I know* what is going on; will *I* do?" It connects to that question Jesus asked the Pharisees, "How can ye believe, which receive honour one of another, and seek not the honour that cometh from God only?" (John 5:44, kjv). If indeed you choose to seek only the honor of God, why not let Him be the only one you tell your grievances to?

When you talk to God, be vulnerable, transparent, and totally honest with Him. Take the mask off. He sees right through you anyway! Don't pretend; don't try to impress

Him. Tell Him your anger, your hurts, and your feeling of bewilderment. The more honest you are, the more intimate will be your relationship with Him. After all, why do you think He let you go through that trial in the first place? It was partly to get your attention. He likes your company. He wants a close relationship with you. The bottom line: it is all because He loves you so much.

2. Make a list of things you are truly thankful for.

When you have been dealt a most severe blow, it is easy to forget the good things you have in life. With effort you can think of some things. The list will grow as you think harder.

I will never forget when I was first convicted over my own ingratitude. It came right in the middle of a sermon—when I was preaching on Philippians 4:6: "Do not be anxious about anything, but in everything, by prayer and petition, *with thanksgiving*, present your requests to God" (emphasis added). The words *with thanksgiving*—which I had read a thousand times before, but that day it was like the first time—made me see how I had taken God for granted, and the many, many things He had done for me. I resolved then and there to be a thankful person from that day on. When I recounted how many things God had done for me but which I never specifically said thank you for, I felt so ashamed. God loves it when we are thankful.

So I strongly recommend you take time to reflect. Go

back over your life. Write down every single thing you are happy about. Did you ever think to say thank you to the Lord? When you do this earnestly and thoughtfully, you will be amazed—and perhaps embarrassed as I was—how long the list becomes.

We had a Sunday prayer meeting every week at Westminster Chapel an hour before the evening service started. We began taking the first fifteen minutes of that prayer meeting to do nothing but thank the Lord for things. I said to them, "No requests. Don't ask Him for anything for fifteen minutes. Just thank Him for things." The first night I put this to the people there was total silence—at first. People didn't know how to begin. So I spoke up: "Thank Him for Jesus. Thank Him for salvation. Thank Him for the Holy Spirit." Those fifteen minutes seemed like an eternity at first. But months later they were that fastest fifteen minutes of that prayer meeting! When you make an effort to recall things you are *sincerely* thankful for, you will be amazed how much there is! As the old hymn put it:

> Count your blessings, name them one by one;
> Count your blessings, see what God hath done!
> Count your blessings, name them one by one;
> And it will surprise you what the Lord hath done.[2]
> —JOHNSON OATMAN, JR. (1897)

3. Fight self-pity and a feeling of entitlement with all your heart.

We come from our mother's womb with a feeling the God owes us something. It is symptomatic of the sin we inherited from the Fall of our first parents in the Garden of Eden that we feel like this. We come into the world not only speaking lies, as we saw, but also feeling that God owes us certain things.

In this book I have had something to say about self-pity and how it is counterproductive in our lives. Closely akin to self-pity is a feeling of entitlement. Modern society has become like this, that the world owes us a living. We likewise transfer this entitlement to God—that He owes us explanations, income, comfort, and, most of all, heaven when we die. The idea that it is of God's mercy that we are not consumed (Lam. 3:22) is alien to us—but is the biblical way of thinking. When Jonathan Edwards preached his sermon from Deuteronomy 32:35, "Their foot shall slide in due time" (KJV), his hearers were shocked but also smitten. Strong men were seen holding on to tree trunks after the service to keep from sliding into hell. For Edwards had said that it was by the mere mercy of God we did not wake up in hell this very day.[3] This kind of thinking is the polar opposite to the way modern man and the contemporary church have been led to believe.

If we will just pause...and think...we will be amazed how much we have to be thankful for. My word to you: tell Him you are thankful. He notices it when we don't thank Him. When Jesus healed ten lepers, only one came back to say thank you. Jesus's response was: "Weren't all ten healed; where are the nine?" God notices it when we are thankful; He notices it when we aren't. (See Luke 17:17.) Make it a habit to tell God of the things you are thankful for. Name them one by one.

4. Choose to believe that God has a purpose in what He has permitted—and thank Him for it.

You may not be convinced yet that He has a purpose in what He has allowed. Don't worry. Joseph could not have known that God had a purpose in his brothers being jealous of him and was behind their decision to sell him to the Ishmaelites.

So with all of us. The worst suffering is the hardest to understand at first. The most natural reaction in the world is to panic and complain. But one day we will see that God was up to something that was very wonderful. As I said earlier, the worst trial of my life was accompanied with the greatest disillusionment and bleakest outlook you can imagine. I can now tell you with total honesty that it was the best thing that ever happened to us. In fact, I would hate to contemplate where we would be today without that trial.

The God of the Bible is a God of purpose. He does nothing accidentally, and all accidents are under His all-seeing eye. The reason that all things work together for good to them that love God is because of God's purpose (Rom. 8:28). His plan. His intent. Joseph said to his brothers, even though they meant to harm him, God meant it for good (Gen. 50:20). God does everything He does according to His sovereign plan; He works everything according to the purpose of His will (Eph. 1:11). If you don't have a robust view of the sovereignty of God, I predict that you will come to this eventually; the sooner, the better. It is the best way to live, namely, knowing that God has a plan for your life. What He said to others centuries ago He says now to you: "'For I know the plans I have for you,' declares the LORD, 'plans to prosper you and not to harm you, plans to give you hope and a future'" (Jer. 29:11).

5. Be patient and willing to wait for things to become clear to you.

Perhaps one of the hardest things of all for us to do is, simply, to wait. "Wait for the LORD; be strong and take heart and wait for the LORD" (Ps. 27:14).

What exactly are you to be waiting for? First, for the dust to settle and for things to become clearer to you. This may take time. It could take a long time. Joseph waited twenty-two years for his dream to be fulfilled. David waited for twenty years before he was made king. During those years he had the anointing but not the crown. Do not be intimidated or envious of those who appear to wear a crown—they are happy and prosperous and perhaps arrogant; it is far better to have the anointing without the crown than the crown without the anointing. As it happens, I waited for twenty-two years before I heard my own dad affirm me. I told him in 1956 I would have an international ministry, thinking it would come any day. But in 1978 as the train was pulling into London's King's Cross station, I actually heard my dad say to me: "Son, you were right and I was wrong; God has indeed been with you, and I am proud of you."

But what if the dust doesn't settle for you and things don't become clear in the present life? This could be the case. I can only say that, if it is, the glory to come is worth waiting for. Jesus endured the cross "for the joy set before him" (Heb. 12:2). It did not come in the days of His life here below. It came later when He was welcomed home to the right hand of God by His Father.

There are some things I don't really expect to be cleared up for me in this life. I gave up a long time ago thinking I would understand this vision, that dream, or the promise I took to be from God. Vindication does not always take place on this earth. We all have to wait for some things to be clear in heaven. Vindication for some will take place in heaven.

Think of the judges that have been bribed, the elections that were rigged, the lies that were believed, and the murders and crimes that were unsolved. Think of the murders that were committed but the innocent person was executed for. Do you think those things were unseen by God? God loves justice. And He will love to vindicate you. Sometimes He does it in the present life; sometimes He waits. But I make you a promise: the longer He waits, the sweeter the vindication will be. I guarantee it. "Therefore judge nothing before the appointed time; wait till the Lord comes. He will bring to light what is hidden in darkness and will expose the motives of men's hearts. At that time each will receive his praise from God" (1 Cor. 4:5).

That, dear reader, is worth waiting for.

CHAPTER ELEVEN

Not Guilty!

I will proclaim the name of the Lord. Oh, praise the greatness of our God! He is the Rock, his works are perfect, and all his ways are just. A faithful God who does no wrong, upright and just is he.

—Deuteronomy 32:3–4

Justice is not always done in this world; we see that every day. But on the Last Day it will be done for all to see. And no one will be able to complain by saying, "This isn't fair."

—D. A. Carson

WHEN I WAS in seminary many years ago, a prominent minister lost his young daughter through an accident. Many talked about it because the minister himself let it be known to everybody that he was bitter. He went to the pulpit to say, "God has a lot to answer for." There is some reason to believe that his daughter's accident led to a change in his theology, which became very liberal and even anti-God.

The thing is, God *will* clear His name one day. But not because He has anything to answer for but because He is the most accused and hated person in the universe. The buck stops with Him, however, and one day He will indeed clear His name. You and I will witness it. Yes, we will all be there, whether we are with those who feel He has a lot to answer for or with those who have cleared His name in advance— by faith.

THE TRUE GOD VERSUS THE COUNTERFEIT GOD

During the same time I was in seminary, we were given a book to read called *God in an Age of Atheism*. I had hoped this book would exalt the true God and show the folly of atheism. But no. It accommodated the atheists of this world so that the author came up with a God that even atheists could believe in. In other words, they didn't need to be atheists after all; the God of the Bible never was or will be the true God. But the author's description of God brought God down to such a level that He was little different from man! It did not describe a God who was omnipotent or a God who knew the future. It reminded me of Paul's words, regarding those people who were given over to a reprobate mind: "They became fools and exchanged the glory of the immortal God for images made to look like mortal man" (Rom. 1:23). The

God described in this book was very like what is known as open theism, the belief (among other things) that God does not infallibly know the future but only the present. According to open theism, not only do we influence Him, but also this God depends on input from us to know what to do next! One of the leading proponents of this theology actually acknowledged publicly that this God may not even win in the end! In any case, if you adopt this kind of God, you can be sure you would not have a need to forgive Him for anything; He doesn't even know any more than you do!

The God of the Bible knows the future—perfectly. "I make known the end from the beginning, from ancient times what is still to come. I say: My purpose will stand and I will do all that I please" (Isa. 46:10). "I am the Alpha and the Omega, the First and the Last, the Beginning and the End" (Rev. 22:13). The reason we have prophecy is because God knows the future as well as He knows the past. How else could Isaiah describe the event of Good Friday with such precision, as though Isaiah 53 was history rather than prophecy? The gospel is based on Habakkuk 2:4; we are made righteous by living by the faithfulness of God. Habakkuk's word speaks of the end and will not prove false. This is why the date of the Second Coming is predestined, already known to God the Father (Matt. 24:36).

And yet the true God is beyond understanding. If we

could understand Him, He would not be God. "Oh, the depth of the riches of the wisdom and knowledge of God! How unsearchable his judgments, and his paths beyond tracing out! Who has known the mind of the Lord? Or who has been his counselor?" (Rom. 11:33–34). We cannot figure Him out, and what He does next is unpredictable. He may repeat Himself in His idiosyncratic fashion—or do what He has never done before.

God Keeps Us in Our Place

And sometimes God shows up in a strange manner, being totally detached and distant. How do you suppose Joshua felt when he saw the messenger of God shortly after the children of Israel entered into the Promised Land? "When Joshua was near Jericho, he looked up and saw a man standing in front of him with a drawn sword in his hand. Joshua went up to him and asked, 'Are you for us or for our enemies?'" The answer: neither. This was no doubt an angel who was the commander of the army of the Lord. (See Joshua 5:13–15.) That army was not visible but unseen by the naked eye. It was the same thing as when Elisha prayed for an anxious man who felt outnumbered by the enemy. "O Lord, open his eyes so he may see. Then the Lord opened the servant's eyes, and he looked and saw the hills full of horses and chariots of fire all around Elisha" (2 Kings 6:17). For Elisha had already told him, "Those who are with us are more than those who are with them" (v. 16). That is what the messenger meant when he said he was commander of the army of the Lord. For God's angelic army was with the children of Israel in their coming battles. The true explanation of their forthcoming victories would not be their military might or ingenious plans but the army of the Lord behind the scenes. Joshua fell facedown. Joshua asked the angel if there was a message for him. The reply: "Take off your sandals, for the place where you are standing is holy" (Josh. 5:15). It was the same instruction as previously given to Moses (Exod. 3:5).

My point is this. The same God who had led the children of Israel up to then—manifesting His glory with the pillar of cloud and fire and manna—was nonetheless *aloof* from Joshua, who said, "Are you for us or your enemies?," the reply being, Neither." Wow. Strange. But God is like that. We are allowed to get close—but only so close. We are invited to have intimacy—but not to the point we get overly familiar with Him. God will always be the God who commands our worship and our respect.

But this is the true God. All-powerful, all-wise, and all-knowing. And faithful. Just. Full of integrity and truth. He cannot lie. He will never fail us; He will never let us down. And yet, ironic as it may seem, "He isn't safe," as C. S. Lewis put it, "but he's good."[1]

Jesus did not worry about being misunderstood. Jesus had a habit of saying very strange things indeed—and not explaining Himself. It was one of His ways. On one occasion He said, "Destroy this temple, and I will raise it again in three days" (John 2:19). He made this statement when He was standing near the temple itself. The Jews retorted, "It has taken forty-six years to build this temple, and are you going to raise it in three days?" (v. 20). Jesus *could* have explained what He meant by that. It would have been so easy for Him to do. But He didn't. He let them think what they would.

That statement of Jesus was used against Him at His trial later on. "This fellow said, 'I am able to destroy the temple of God and rebuild it in three days'" (Matt. 26:61). That, by the way, is *not* what Jesus said; He said He would raise it again in three days. "Then the high priest stood up and said to Jesus, 'Are you not going to answer? What is this testimony that these men are bringing against you?' But Jesus remained silent" (Matt. 26:62–63). He could have explained Himself, but He didn't. Hours later—when He was hanging on the cross—they used it against Jesus again. They hurled insults at Him, "You who are going to destroy the temple and build it in three days, save yourself! Come down from the cross, if you are the Son of God!" (Matt. 27:40). He could have explained Himself, but He didn't. Why not? The answer is:

to see who would persist in faith when they heard Jesus say things that didn't seem to make sense.

This example of Jesus not explaining Himself is typical of God's ways. What Jesus said seemed so outrageous—that He would raise the temple in three days. Nothing was so obvious to bystanders, then, that Jesus was not to be trusted. Those insulting Him as He was on the cross felt as safe as if in their mothers arms when they said what they did. Jesus appeared to be a complete fraud.

This, then, is how most people are today with God. To them it is so obvious that God is not to be trusted. For if He is to be trusted, He would surely explain Himself so we could believe in Him, most would think. The greatest freedom is having nothing to prove. The God of the Bible has nothing to prove.

There is another similar incident in which Jesus said mystifying things that made no sense. First, He claimed to be the very bread that came down from heaven in Moses's day. Despite His having fed five thousand people with two small fish and five small barley loaves, they asked, "What miraculous sign then will you give that we may see it and believe you?" (John 6:9–13, 30). Imagine that! Having seen a miraculous sign, they were still asking Him to do a miraculous sign! This goes to show that when people demand a miracle to prove the validity of the God of the Bible or the Bible itself, such a miracle will not satisfy them. Only the Holy Spirit will enable a person to believe fully in the Scriptures. These people went on to say that their forefathers ate the manna in the desert, quoting Exodus 16:4: "He gave them bread from heaven to eat" (John 6:31). Jesus said a most audacious thing to them: "I am the bread that came down from heaven" (v. 41). Whoa! They really thought they had a gotcha situation then! How would Jesus get out of that one? But Jesus did not explain what He meant.

But there was more. He called himself the bread of life, adding that "this bread is my flesh, which I will give for the life of the world" (v. 51). The hearers began to argue sharply among themselves, "How can this man gives us his flesh to eat?" (v. 52). Jesus did not bother to answer, much less to explain Himself. He could have, but He didn't. And if that were not enough, Jesus delivered to them the irrefutable evidence and the crowning excuse they might be looking for in order to dismiss all His claims:

> I tell you the truth, unless you eat the flesh of the Son of Man and drink his blood, you have no life in you. Whoever eats my flesh and drinks my blood has eternal life, and I will raise him up at the last day. For my flesh is real food and my blood is real drink. Whoever eats my flesh and drinks my blood remains in me, and I in him. Just as the living Father sent me and I live because of the Father, so the one who feeds on me will

live because of me. This is the bread that came down from heaven. Your forefathers ate manna and died, but he who feeds on this bread will live forever.

—JOHN 6:53–58

Jesus could have explained what He meant by these words, but He didn't. Why not? The answer is: *to see who will persist in faith* after being dealt a severe blow that might undermine all they had believed up to now. Like it or not, Jesus put obstacles in their way. You may have thought that God was hard up for a following. You may have thought Jesus was trying to build an empire by which He could impress the Romans. Wrong.

But what He did by saying these seemingly ridiculous things—as people eating His flesh and drinking His blood—worked. Did it ever! The initial response was, "This is a hard teaching. Who can accept it?" (John 6:60). The fallout of Jesus's preaching in John 6—despite His feeding five thousand—was this: "*From this time* many of his disciples turned back and no longer followed him" (v. 66, emphasis added).

Five thousand down to twelve! Could this be the typical proportionate percentage of those who feel let down by God vis-à-vis those who persist in faith? I don't know. I do, however, recall Jesus's words regarding those who take the narrow way to life: "Only a few find it" (Matt. 7:14).

At that time Jesus turned to the Twelve who were still hanging around. "'You do not want to leave too, do you?'... Simon Peter answered him, 'Lord, to whom shall we go? You have the words of eternal life. We believe and know that you are the Holy One of God'" (John 6:67–68).

Peter's answer is the answer we all should embrace. It is what persistent faith is all about. Peter didn't know one bit more than the thousands who deserted Jesus. He was not more intelligent, was not better educated, and had no more inside information as to the meaning of those strange, if not bizarre, words about eating Jesus's flesh and drinking His blood. But he said, "I'm staying put. I'm not leaving. I don't understand what You are saying, but I am staying with You, Jesus. In any case, where would I go? To whom shall we go?" Peter did not make his decision on what Jesus had done for him. He was not better off physically or financially. He did not get his questions answered. He based everything upon the Word: "You have the words of eternal life" (v. 68).

That is all Peter had going for him. The Word. Jesus's Word. "I don't understand it, but I believe it," Peter was virtually saying.

That is persistent faith. You and I are not given a higher IQ or special education by which we can grasp the Bible. We don't have inside information as to the real answer to the problem of evil and suffering. We have a lot of questions. They remain unanswered. But we have the Bible. It has not let us down. We know we are on solid ground here. What we have is pure gold.

It was John, not Jesus, who explained what Jesus meant by the temple. John added an editorial comment: "But the temple he had spoken of was his *body*. After he was raised from the dead, his disciples recalled what he said. Then they believed the Scripture and the words that Jesus had spoken" (John 2:21–22, emphasis added). As to the meaning of eating Jesus's flesh and drinking His blood, this of course referred to the Eucharist, the Lord Supper, Holy Communion. We all take this for granted now. But then it was a case of trusting Jesus's words without understanding their meaning.

When God clears His name, it will be as simple as that. Nobody could have guessed that Jesus's reference to the temple was His body. Nobody could have figured out that Jesus's reference to eating flesh and drinking blood was the Lord's Supper. It is obvious now, but it wasn't then.

God is like that. He reveals enough of Himself to create faith—which saves us—but not so much that we know everything! It is persistent faith that follows saving faith. "So then, just as you received Christ Jesus as Lord, continue to live in him, rooted and built up in him, strengthened in the faith as you were taught, and overflowing with thankfulness" (Col. 2:6–7).

WHAT WILL THAT DAY BE LIKE?

One day things will be made plain to us.

> Someday He'll make it plain to me,
> Someday when I His face shall see;
> Someday from tears I shall be free,
> For someday I shall understand.[2]

What will it be like on that day when God clears His name? I only know that I can hardly wait! The wonderful thing is—this blows me away: I will be there. So will you. What a moment it will be! Will we cry? Will we laugh? Will we shout? Will we hug each other like we have never done before? Or will we say anything at all, but only be taking it in and finding out for sure—surprise, surprise—that we were on the winning side from the moment we received Jesus Christ as our Savior and Lord.

Yes. God will win. Not only that; it will be manifest and without doubt that the God who made us, the God who sent Jesus, the God who saved us, and the God who kept us is...not guilty! We will shout it with all our hearts in loud voices, "Not guilty!" The patriarchs of the Old Testament—Abraham, Isaac, and Jacob—will shout, "Not guilty!" David, Hezekiah, and Josiah will be singing, "Not guilty!" Isaiah, Jeremiah, Ezekiel, and Habakkuk will be shouting, "Not guilty!" The martyrs of the early church will shout, "Not guilty!" The angels—the cherubim and seraphim—will join in singing, "Not guilty!"

That's not all. We who have not had our questions answered but chose to trace the rainbow through the rain will shout, "Not guilty!" All those who suffered and experienced extreme injustice and who were at one time on the brink of giving up—but persisted instead—will cry out with unimaginable joy, "Not guilty!" Every knee shall bow and every tongue shall confess that Jesus Christ is Lord to the glory of God the Father and will exclaim, "Not guilty!"

Read the last book of the Bible—the Book of Revelation. I don't completely understand that book (and I don't know who does), but one thing is clear: God wins, the devil loses, and we who have overcome by the blood of the Lamb will see the most glorious vindication of all time! It will be God's vindication. It will be for real. It will be final. There will be no higher court. And no one will say, "This isn't fair."

CHAPTER TWELVE

A Dream Deferred

Though the fig tree does not bud and there are no grapes on the vines, though the olive crop fails and the fields produce no food, though there are no sheep in the pen and no cattle in the stalls, yet I will rejoice in the LORD, I will be joyful in God my Savior.

—HABAKKUK 3:17–18

Hope deferred makes the heart sick, but a longing fulfilled is a tree of life.

—PROVERBS 13:12

What happens to a dream deferred? Does it dry up like a raisin in the sun? Or fester like a sore—and then run? Does it stink like rotten meat? Or crust and sugar over—like a syrupy sweet? Maybe it just sags like a heavy load. Or does it explode?

—LANGSTON HUGHES (1902–1967)

WHAT DO YOU do when you don't get what you want? And what if it becomes obvious you *never* will have it in this present life? What is

215

the next step forward, then, when you come to terms with the dreaded fact that your prayer *isn't* going to be answered, your wish *isn't* going to be fulfilled, and even what you thought *God* promised isn't going to come through for you?

But there is another situation; it is when it is absolutely certain that your promise will come to fruition—*but not yet.* When you hold on to faith in God at such a time, you have just been upgraded to the category of Abraham. You may recall that he was promised Canaan as a possession but did not get any inheritance there whatever, not even a foot of ground (Acts 7:5). So you are in good company! You are also elevated to the rank of those people described in Hebrews 11:39 who "were all commended for their faith, yet none of them received what had been promised."

But what else can we say about Abraham? Dr. Michael Eaton says it is a *biblical principle* that when God promises something but it does not apparently come, you are given a temporary substitute—which is, in fact, far better than what you initially wanted. Joni Eareckson Tada's worldwide ministry was the temporary substitute for her being healed, which she had prayed for. Paul's thorn in the flesh was not removed, but he was compensated by grace far greater than the thorn (2 Cor. 12:9)! The principle that glory outweighs troubles (2 Cor. 4:17) is always in play when we don't get what we want but persist in faith. So when we don't get the reconciliation we wanted, we are forced to live on God's approval—which is better than the reconciliation. The nightmarish marriage, moreover, may lead you to an unusual relationship with God—which is far better than the unhappy marriage.

This was the case with every single person described in Hebrews 11. They all accomplished extraordinary things— the temporary substitute—because they believed the promise, persisting in faith. When Abraham did not get the land he was promised, he was given a substitute—Isaac—whose seed was actually Jesus Christ (Gal. 3:16). As for the land that he did not inherit, he was looking for the city with foundations, that is, heaven (Heb. 11:8–10). Jeremiah said, "Ah, Sovereign Lord, how completely you have deceived this people" (Jer. 4:10). And God replied that things would get even worse (Jer. 12:5–14). But that is not the end of the story. God replied that He had intervened for Jeremiah's good (Jer. 15:11)—a man whose words form a book in the canon of Scripture and who was personally vindicated by history.

In this final chapter, we return one more time to the prophet Habakkuk—our hero. Wow. What a man. He did not get what he wanted. He first wanted an explanation as to how God could allow evil. His second complaint was to ask: How could the most holy God raise up the wicked Babylonians—Judah's ancient enemy—to sort out His own covenant people? Nothing added up. Nothing made sense.

However, Habakkuk did not give up. He persisted. He said he would stand and wait for God to show up, believing as he did that God would answer. *And God did answer.* However, it was not what Habakkuk was expecting or wanting. Hardly. But because it was God Himself speaking, the prophet Habakkuk took it—and applied it.

The answer was: the revelation, namely, the meaning of what is going on, would be coming down the road. "It speaks of the *end* and will not prove false. Though it linger, wait for it; it will certainly come and will not delay" (Hab. 2:3, emphasis added). The Lord's answer hints of kicking the can down the road—buying more time. However, God was not asking for more time; it was given to show the plan of salvation! Those who would rely on God's faithfulness would get their explanation—down the road, yes, but in the meantime they are *saved.* They live *by God's integrity*; they truly believe His promise. Those therefore who do this are declared righteous—as Abraham was: the righteous will live by God's faithfulness. Living by God's faithfulness is exactly what faith is. You have no evidence, only His Word. You are totally relying on His promise to come through for you.

And what do you suppose was Habakkuk's response to this? Did he say, "No, that is not good enough"? Not at all. He accepted it from the crown of his head to the soles of his feet. The affect this had on Habakkuk was his inflexible resolve; it contains some of the most sublime and moving words in all Holy Writ. It is sometimes hard for me to read this word without coming to tears:

> Though the fig tree does not bud and there are no grapes on the vines, though the olive crop fails and the fields produce no food, though there are no sheep in the pen and no cattle in the stalls, yet I will rejoice in the Lord, I will be joyful in God my Savior.
> —Habakkuk 3:17–18

Keep in mind that Habakkuk lived in an agrarian society. They depended daily on the crops, fruit, cattle, sheep—not to mention sunshine and rain—for survival. The prophet Habakkuk becomes our example. Like the new Joseph we saw earlier, so too Habakkuk; he is a changed man. He practices what he preaches. If there was no food, fruit, or sustenance for tomorrow, he would rejoice. If his specific wish was not granted, he would be joyful. Habakkuk had said he would wait for God's word. He got it; he accepted it. It gave him a new resolve. Disappointed though he was—this being a promise to *wait*—he embraced it with his whole being.

What about you and me? Will we persist in faith even though we are not going to get what we want?

David said that if you delight in the Lord, He would give you the desires of your heart (Ps. 37:4). But—just suppose—you *have* delighted yourself in the Lord, but He has *not* given you the desires of your heart. What then?

I also have to ask myself this question—all the time: If my desires are not His desires for me, would I still want them? I answer: no. Disappointed though I am, I embrace this faithful and inflexible truth: God only wants what is best for me. "No good thing does he withhold from those whose walk is blameless" (Ps. 84:11). Psalm 37:4 presupposes that our delighting *in the Lord* means that it is only *His* desires we—ultimately—truly want. Since God only wants what is best for us, would we truly persist in demanding what He does not want us to have? So there comes a time you concede that what you wanted must not have been His idea—His will—after all. Never forget this basic assumption that God only hears us when we ask according to His will (1 John 5:14).

What if, therefore—should this be the case with you—that you now accept that:

- Your most earnest prayer will not be answered

- You won't get healed

- You won't get married

- You won't get the reconciliation you wanted

- The revival—or the awakening—that you hoped for won't come

- You won't have children

- Those people won't forgive you but will always hold the grudge

- That faulty verdict from the uncaring judge won't be reversed

- That enigmatic situation that has bedeviled you will remain a puzzle

- You will go to your grave unvindicated—everyone believes those lies

- War is coming; terrorism has spread, and it cannot be stopped

- There will be no clarification of certain verses in the Bible

- The prophecy given to you will remain unfulfilled

- That disability you have lived with won't go away

- Your nightmarish marriage will continue on and on

- You won't get the job you wanted

- You won't get to live in the home of your dreams

WHAT NEXT?

What, then, is the possibility that you can—from your heart—echo Habakkuk's response in the light of his deferred dream:

> Though the fig tree does not bud and there are no
> grapes on the vines, though the olive crop fails and
> the fields produce no food, though there are no sheep
> in the pen and no cattle in the stalls, yet I will rejoice
> in the Lord, I will be joyful in God my Savior.
>
> —Habakkuk 3:17–18

As we approach the end of this book, I ask you: Can you agree with what Habakkuk says above? If your purpose in reading this book was because you have been *upset with God* but can now honestly echo Habakkuk's words, my mission in writing this book is accomplished. That is the best proof of totally forgiving God I can think of. After all, it is God who makes the fig tree bud; it is God who is in control of these things that Habakkuk mentions. It is God's prerogative to give or withhold mercy (Rom. 9:15). If then you don't get what you want but you can honestly and sincerely repeat Habakkuk's words from your heart, you have set God free; you have let Him off the hook. That is what totally forgiving God is.

WHOM DO YOU BLAME WHEN
YOU DON'T UNDERSTAND?

I recently watched John Piper's brilliant interview with Rick Warren, famed author of *The Purpose-Driven Life*. Rick Warren said that "any apparent contradiction in Scripture, is my limited capacity."[1] That to me is the quintessence of breaking the betrayal barrier. Don't blame God. Consider that the inability to grasp what we don't understand lies in us. As noted above, Abraham as well as all those described in Hebrews 11 did not get what was promised, but they persisted in faith nonetheless. They did not blame God. Habakkuk did not get what he wanted, but he persisted in faith. He even said he would *rejoice.*

CAN YOU DO THIS?

There comes a time when faith is a choice we make. Whereas faith is God's gracious gift—this being the evidence of divine favor (Eph. 2:8–9)—we nonetheless make a choice whether or not to affirm the God of the Bible. Habakkuk said he would rejoice despite things not turning out so well. One must make a choice to rejoice. Total forgiveness is an act of the will. Totally forgiving ourselves is a choice we must make. Totally forgiving God is what we do not because we get our questions answered but because we choose to trust God's integrity. Dear reader, it is the safest choice you will ever make.

Sometimes God *does* eventually give hints along the way—instead of making us wait until we get to heaven—as to why things happen that make no sense at the time. You may recall that Uzzah died for touching the ark of the covenant. Why, then, did Uzzah die because he merely reached out to steady the ark as it was being brought into Jerusalem? David eventually found out. King David, whose idea it was to bring the ark into Jerusalem in the first place—this being a godly, noble gesture—was initially *angry* because of what the Lord did. But he soon cooled off and became afraid of the Lord (2 Sam. 6:7–9). Not that he understood why God did this (at first); he merely persisted in faith. Sometime later he found out what had actually gone wrong. "We did not inquire of him how to do it in the prescribed way" (1 Chron. 15:13). The Levitical Law (in Exodus, Leviticus, Numbers) had made it perfectly clear how the ark should be carried, but no one took it seriously. This account is an indication that there is a always a hidden reason for what God does or doesn't do. If God reveals that reason before long, good. That revelation is always sweet to have. But if God *doesn't* reveal the reason here on earth, remember Job: "Though he slay me, yet will I hope in him" (Job 13:15).

I sometimes find it almost amusing that Jesus did not bother to explain Himself when He made what seemed at the time the most outlandish statements. As we saw above, He said to the Jews, "Destroy this temple, and I will raise it again in three days." *Really?* You will recall that the Jews replied, "It has taken forty-six years to build this temple, and you are going to raise it in three days?" (John 2:19–20). Jesus did not say a word to them, much less did He bother to explain what He meant. And sure enough, this statement was used against Him at His trial before the Sanhedrin (Matt. 26:61). Jesus did not explain what He meant to the Jewish officials either but remained silent. If He were like most of us, He would have explained what He meant lest people think He was crazy! Jesus deliberately chose to make Himself of no reputation (Phil. 2:5–7, KJV). The same is true with His hard saying, "Unless you eat the flesh of the Son of Man and drink his blood, you have no life in you" (John 6:53). He did not try to hold His following together by explaining, "I am actually referring to Holy Communion— which you will understand after I die and am raised from the dead." No. It was an opportunity to see who among His following would persist in faith without understanding what He meant.

I would lovingly suggest to you that when you don't understand certain scriptures, you ascribe it to your "limited capacity," as Rick Warren put it. I have questions too, by the way. I don't understand why God created hell and lets people go there. I don't understand why He allows them be born in the first place when He—who knows the future as well as the past—realizes they will eventually go to hell. Furthermore, I don't know why God doesn't *save* everybody. I don't know why He won't take everybody to heaven. I would (if He left it to me). Yes, I have questions too. But

I always remember the verse Mrs. Martyn Lloyd-Jones said she leaned on in this connection: "Will not the Judge of all the earth do right?" (Gen. 18:25). I can live with that.

Abraham did not know what God meant when he was ordered to sacrifice his only son, Isaac (Gen. 22:2). It absolutely made no sense. But Abraham obeyed. He surmised that God would merely raise Isaac from the dead (Heb. 11:19). That was not the way it turned out, but Abraham was willing to leave it all to God. His reward after that momentous decision to trust God's integrity was too great to put into words.

I can promise you this: if you will totally forgive God by *believing* Him and *waiting*, you will eventually discover that He meant it for good—whatever it was you have been through. Michael Eaton reckons that the theme of forgiving God is the *God meant it for good* principle heightened to a global-universal-astronomical level. Indeed, the temporary enigma always heightens the final solution!

So therefore with you and me. God has chosen *faith* as the way by which He would be known. It is the road less traveled, as Robert Frost's poem put it. And taking that road will indeed make all the difference. Those who believe will—eventually—be richly rewarded. Therefore those who follow Habakkuk's example will—eventually—be vindicated. When He *does* reward us along the way—by giving us visible tokens of His grace here below—it pleases *us* no end!

Quite. I wish it would happen every day. But when we live by His integrity and faithfulness—without getting our questions answered—it pleases *Him* no end. The eventual reward is incalculable.

Faith then is our opportunity to please Him (Heb. 11:6). There will be no faith in heaven. Now is the precious time during which we can demonstrate valiantly before Him, the world, and the angels that we unashamedly believe in the God of the Bible.

May God Almighty—Father, Son, and Holy Spirit—bless you, keep you, sustain you, and preserve you now and evermore. Amen.

NOTES

Introduction

1. John F. Kennedy Library and Museum, "John F. Kennedy Quotations," http://www.jfklibrary.org/Research/Ready -Reference/JFK-Quotations.aspx (accessed March 6, 2012).

Chapter One—The Dilemma

1. BrainyQuote, "Saint Augustine Quotes," http://www .brainyquote.com/quotes/quotes/s/saintaugus148527.html (accessed March 6, 2012).

2. "Jesus, Lover of My Soul" by Charles Wesley. Public domain.

3. Quotationpark.com, "David Livingstone Quotes," http://www .quotationpark.com/authors/LIVINGSTONE,%20David.html (accessed March 6, 2012).

Chapter Two—Habakkuk's Complaints

1. Samuel Butler, *Hudibras*, part iii, canto iii, line 547.

2. Beliefnet.com, "Inspirational Quotes," http://tinyurl .com/6mh6wla (accessed March 7, 2012).

3. "Someday He'll Make It Plain" by Lydia S. Leech. Public domain.

Chapter Three—Let Down

1. Thinkexist.com, "Winston Churchill Quotes," http://thinkexist. com/quotation/never-never-never-never_give_up/15825.html (accessed March 7, 2012).

2. "Be Thankful: Studies Show Having Gratitude Can Improve Your Health," *Tampa Bay Times*, http://www.tampabay.com/ news/health/article966880.ece (accessed March 7, 2012).

Chapter Four—Why Faith?

1. YogiBerra.com, "Yogi-isms," http://www.yogiberra.com/yogi -isms.html (accessed March 8, 2012).

2. "O Love That Wilt Not Let Me Go" by George Matheson. Public domain.

Chapter Six—God's Reply to Habakkuk

1. *The Apologetics Study Bible* (Nashville, TN: Holman Bible Publishers, 2007).

2. Ibid.

3. Ibid.

Chapter Eight—Deceitful Hearts

1. Thinkexist.com, "Charles H. Spurgeon Quotes," http://thinkexist.com/quotation/beware_of_no_man_more_than_of_yourself-we_carry/260515.html (accessed March 8, 2012).

Chapter Nine—Why Forgive God?

1. Thinkexist.com, "C.S. Lewis Quotes," http://thinkexist.com/quotation/aim_at_heaven_and_you_will_get_earth_thrown_in/201460.html (accessed March 8, 2012).

2. Thinkexist.com, "Alexander Pope Quotes," http://thinkexist.com/quotation/to_err_is_human-to_forgive_divine/10168.html (accessed March 8, 2012).

Chapter Ten—How to Forgive God—Totally

1. "Stronger Than Before" by Janny Grein. Copyright © 1988 Mighty Wind Music. ASCAP.

2. "Count Your Blessings" by Johnson Oatman Jr.. Public domain.

3. Jonathan Edwards, "Sinners in the Hands of an Angry God," Christian Classics Ethereal Library, http://www.ccel.org/ccel/edwards/sermons.sinners.html (accessed March 8, 2012).

Chapter Eleven—Not Guilty!

1. C. S. Lewis, *The Lion, the Witch, and the Wardrobe* (New York: HarperCollins Publishers Inc., 1998), 99.

2. "Someday He'll Make It Plain" by Lydia S. Leech. Public domain.

Chapter Twelve—A Dream Deferred

1. Saddleback Valley Community Church, Interview With Pastor Rick Warren and Pastor John Piper, May 1, 2011, http://www.scribd.com/doc/55821766/John-Piper-Interview-Pastor-Rick-Warren-Transcript (accessed March 8, 2012).

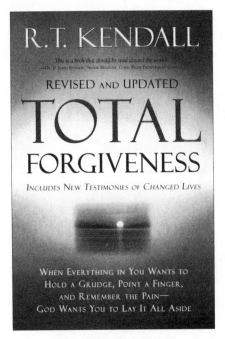
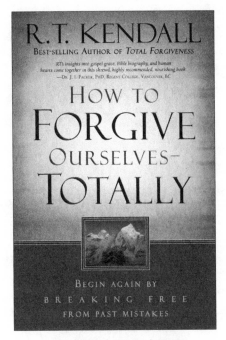